HAUNTED HAMILTON

The Ghosts of Dundurn Castle
and Other Steeltown Shivers

HAUNTED HAMILTON

MARK LESLIE

DUNDURN
TORONTO

Copy Editor: Matt Baker
Design: Courtney Horner
Printer: Webcom

Library and Archives Canada Cataloguing in Publication

Leslie, Mark, 1969-
    Haunted Hamilton : the ghosts of Dundurn Castle and other Steeltown shivers / Mark Leslie.

Issued also in electronic formats.
ISBN 978-1-4597-0401-5

    1. Ghosts--Ontario--Hamilton. 2. Haunted places--Ontario--Hamilton. 3. Ghost stories, Canadian (English). I. Title.

BF1472.C3L47 2012   133.109713'52   C2012-903194-1

3 4 5   21 20 19

Conseil des Arts du Canada   Canada Council for the Arts   Canadä   ONTARIO ARTS COUNCIL   CONSEIL DES ARTS DE L'ONTARIO

We acknowledge the support of the **Canada Council for the Arts** and the **Ontario Arts Council** for our publishing program. We also acknowledge the financial support of the **Government of Canada** through the **Canada Book Fund** and **Livres Canada Books**, and the **Government of Ontario** through the **Ontario Book Publishing Tax Credit** and the **Ontario Media Development Corporation.**

Care has been taken to trace the ownership of copyright material used in this book. The author and the publisher welcome any information enabling them to rectify any references or credits in subsequent editions.

J. Kirk Howard, President

Printed and bound in Canada.
www.dundurn.com

Author photo courtesy of Peter Rainford
Images courtesy of Peter Rainford and Stephanie Lechniak

Dundurn	Gazelle Book Services Limited	Dundurn
3 Church Street, Suite 500	White Cross Mills	2250 Military Road
Toronto, Ontario, Canada	High Town, Lancaster, England	Tonawanda, NY
M5E 1M2	LA1 4XS	U.S.A. 14150

For Mom,

*Thanks for always keeping me safe from the ghosts
and the monsters under my bed*

Few things become architecture so well as a whiff of the past and a hint of the uncanny. Canada needs ghosts, as a dietary supplement, a vitamin taken to stave off that most dreadful of modern ailments, the Rational Rickets.

— Robertson Davies, *High Spirits*

REMEMBER FRIEND, AS YOU PASS BY

AS YOU ARE NOW SO ONCE WAS I

AS I AM NOW, SO YOU WILL BE

PREPARE FOR DEATH AND FOLLOW ME

— Epitaph on a tombstone in Burkholder Cemetery, Hamilton, Ontario

CONTENTS

A FOREWORD IN TWO PARTS

By Daniel Cumerlato and Stephanie Lechniak

Hamilton: A Town of Character, Communities, and Creepy History

Hamilton is our home. Both Stephanie and I were raised in the city. I am originally an east-ender and Stephanie is a Mountain girl. We were from two different worlds, but we are both Hamiltonians. Everything about who we are started here, in the Ambitious City we call home.

Hamilton has long been in the shadow of Toronto. Perhaps for a few years back in the 1850s, Hamiltonians thought they would surpass Toronto, but the idea quickly faded into the dust of modernism. Since the late 1800s, we've tried to be a big city, with big city dreams, but in the end the citizens decided there was no use fighting. We are a town of character and communities.

It's this character that gives the city its appealing history; a history connected to its ghosts.

We first got into the paranormal, ironically, while living in Toronto for a year. For fun, we bought a fifty-cent Ouija board from a garage sale and contacted the dead with our first-ever taped session that same night. The board didn't move much, but afterwards, when listening to the microcassette recorder, we found a very clear EVP (Electrical Voice Phenomenon, or ghost voice). When we asked, "Spirit, are you there?" a breathy voice, distinct and loud, as if located right up against the microphone, had answered — *yes*.

We posted this experience on the Internet and were contacted by some TV producers. Nothing came of the EVP, but it was during this interview that we first heard about the notorious "murder house" in Hamilton. The producers freely talked about the ghosts, legends, and violent history of this mysterious house on Hamilton Mountain, but didn't tell us the address, for fear we might use it before they had a chance to. A couple of days later, we were standing in front of Bellevue Mansion, the murder house, located at the west end of Concession Street.

I was never much of a history buff as a child. To me, history was a subject in school, not something you could experience in person. After returning to Hamilton with Stephanie, this all changed.

We took many pictures of Bellevue. After staring at the pile of pictures and all of our research, we decided the story needed to be told. So began Haunted Hamilton. Bellevue Mansion was demolished about a year later in the dead of night by a greedy landowner. Our pictures of the house were the last ever taken.

We were hooked. Stephanie and I set out to discover as many historically haunted locations as possible: the Custom House, Hermitage Ruins, Auchmar Mansion, Whitehern Mansion, Albion Falls, and of course Dundurn Castle were all places we would visit over the next year. It was during this time that Haunted Hamilton transformed into a public hub for ghost stories, but also a place for celebrating Hamilton's unique history, which complements the many ghosts who haunt it. Our past is not a story of success through white-collared games, but instead the blood and sweat of blue-collar workers. This gives the city a rough exterior and the permanent role of underdog.

Our stories are infused with romance, mystery, and intrigue. Our history is bred in violence and pioneered by fighters who envisioned a city while staring down at a jungle. We've experienced war, murder, and mobsters — all the while trying hard to compete with the growing demands of an emerging nation. Nothing stopped, the city formed, and it's that determination that gives Hamilton its ghosts.

Our many years of ghost-hunting experience have changed the way we look at history. The many paranormal occurrences we have already experienced seem like an open invitation for even more strange happenings; as if the ghosts are talking about us behind our backs, saying, "Those guys are in the know, let's talk to them" and giving us a personal connection to the past.

We would become ready for them, especially on nights before an investigation. One such night, before investigating a four-year-old townhouse, stays with us.

I was sleeping and Stephanie was in the living room. It was near Christmas, and we had our tree set up in the dining room. Stephanie heard squeaking noises and watched our two cats run over to stare at the tree, just before it fell against the window. When Stephanie checked the base, she saw that the four large steel bolts had come loose all by themselves.

She ran into the bedroom and told me the entire story. After calming her, we both went to sleep. That same night, I had two vivid dreams. In the first, I saw Stephanie turn around in bed and start talking to me in a foreign language. To this day, I'm not familiar with what language was spoken, but I'll never forget the strange way she was smiling at me.

The second dream had me walking into an empty bedroom with the lights on. The curtains were open, exposing the large windows, and — in the reflection only — I could see a tall man standing on the bed, wearing a long coat with a wide-brimmed hat covering his face. This would be my first meeting with "the Jesuit," a ghost we would all be familiar with by the end of the investigation.

At no point during this experience did we see a physical apparition while awake; however, we know fully this was a ghostly experience.

In the over ten years of running Haunted Hamilton, Stephanie and I can claim only one time each when we actually saw a ghost. This does not include hearing footsteps on the second floor, feeling the presence of something not visible to the naked eye, capturing an orb, or having something disappear; what I'm talking about is the experience of a visual manifestation of a spirit.

For me it was at the Hermitage Ruins in Ancaster. We were finishing up the Ghost Walk, when I walked around the ruins to tell people it was time to leave. After clearing the side wall of the ruins, I saw two people walking away from me. I called to them but neither stopped. I called a second time, and both of them walked into the forest. I ran quickly, only seconds behind, to an area covered with bushes and many tripping hazards. I shone the flashlight into the woods to find that both people had vanished.

For Stephanie, it happened while cleaning up after a Ghost Walk at the Custom House in Hamilton's historic North End. Sitting in the main lobby, she was carefully scraping wax off of a table, when she heard footsteps. She looked up to see nobody was there, but the footsteps continued as if an invisible person were walking down the middle aisle toward her. She froze, afraid, staring out over the rows of chairs into the empty gallery. Then, for just a split second, a woman appeared, sitting properly stick-straight in one of the aisle chairs. She was looking directly at Stephanie. Then, as fast as the woman appeared, she was gone.

Stephanie and I have always considered ourselves journalists in the field. We never become too much of a believer or a skeptic when it comes to the unknown.

Believe too much and you'll find amazing amounts of unproven evidence. Believe too little and you'll never see or experience anything. Stay on the fence to watch the expert psychics, mediums, scientists, and photographers do their trade in the most haunted locations, and you'll end up with an amazing view from the sky, looking down to find common factors.

Failing that, there's always a great ghost story as a personal link to history. It's something to experience and never ignore, something to revel in and enjoy, and something, if you're lucky, that just may scare you.

Daniel Cumerlato
Founding Partner of Haunted Hamilton Ghost Walks & Events

Of Notepads, Haunted Houses, and Thresholds to the Unknown

From the moment we stepped through the threshold, we knew our lives had changed forever; we entered the Bellevue Mansion as kids, merely nineteen and twenty-one years old, yet emerged over a decade later as grown adults, in our thirties, still fascinated with the unusual and things that go bump in the night. That beautiful, sunny day in September of 2000 was a special moment in time — a day when we learned how to appreciate history and the abundance of it right here in our own backyard.

Now, twelve years later, we fondly remember back to when we first began Haunted Hamilton. The Bellevue Mansion was our inspiration at a time when our eyes were closed to the world of the paranormal. I was attending a new media design school in Toronto, and Daniel was working the daily grind at a computer company as an IT analyst.

Our weekdays were pretty hectic, and one early Saturday morning we decided to go to some garage sales. Oddly enough, we had found ourselves at an old funeral home in downtown Hamilton that was having a community sale in the parking lot outside. And there it was ... an old, beaten-up Ouija board from the 1980s. We dusted it off and asked, "How much?" The old man at the table was eager to give it to us for only fifty cents, so we happily paid and left with what that we thought was only a cheap board game.

Several weeks later, we finally pulled the board out and gave it a whirl, but we were both unsure how to use it. The only experience I had was as a little girl, playing with my girlfriends at a birthday party. So when Daniel and I first placed our fingertips on the planchette, we weren't sure what to expect.

After some jokes and silly comments, the board started to work! The planchette started pointing to letters and numbers not making any sense at all, until it began to spell out, U R A HAPPY COUPLE. At that moment, I began to cry, and Daniel just looked at me in shock. We both had a strong trust in each other, enough to know it wasn't a joke and that neither of us had spelled it out intentionally.

A few months later, we decided to step it up a notch. We rested a microcassette recorder (yes, it was that long ago — before there were these fancy digital ones!) on the table beside the board and started to communicate. Our first question was, "Is there a spirit present?" and the planchette pointed to the word YES. It was an all-around successful session, so we closed it off by saying goodbye to the spirit, then sat back and rewound the tape.

There it was ... something that opened our eyes and solidified our view of the paranormal. It was a life-changing moment. After we had asked if there was a spirit present, we clearly heard a voice responding back into the microphone, loudly whispering *yes-s-s*. From that moment on, we were hooked. We were hooked, intrigued by the strange, the unusual, and most of all, by ghosts and spirits on the other side.

And this is what eventually led us to the "murder house" in Hamilton, where our story truly begins, standing at the precipice of this enormous, empty edifice known as Bellevue, with the sun peering through the cracks in the plywood that blocked the windows. It was almost beckoning, welcoming us to enter; we both felt a strong sense of purpose just being there.

With my dad's trusty 35mm camera around my neck and several rolls of film on hand, we ventured into the Bellevue Mansion. Along with a historical write-up, the photos I snapped would become the very first article on our newly designed website, which we called Haunted Hamilton.

Strangely enough, here I am countless years later, looking for a notepad to write my thoughts down for this foreword, when I find an old, dusty notebook in my cabinet. I start to flip through the pages and realize it is our very first notebook, where we penned our dreams, hopes, game plans, and ideas for Haunted Hamilton. The interesting part? Not much has changed. Even when we were kids, we were still passionate about the wondrous history of our city. It was over a decade ago when we wrote about the need for restoration, preservation, and educating Hamiltonians (and tourists alike) about this unique city of ours — the Ambitious City, as it was often referred to as over a hundred years ago.

This old notebook couldn't have been found at a more perfect time. Reading through the pages reminded me of just how far we have come and in what ways, how we still feel so compelled to share Hamilton's unique stories and tales with everyone.

From the Dark Lady, who famously haunts the old Custom House on Stuart Street, to the legend of William Black, the lonely coachman whose spirit still wanders the woods at the Hermitage Ruins in Ancaster, Hamilton is *alive* with ghosts from the past. A decade's worth of research isn't enough. There is still a world of stories, legends, and folklore waiting to be told. This book is your ultimate guide to uncover the unique and historically haunted treasures in our city: read through it, learn, explore, and get up close and personal with the ghosts of Haunted Hamilton.

Stephanie Lechniak,
Founding Partner of Haunted Hamilton Ghost Walks & Events

ACKNOWLEDGEMENTS

I owe an extreme gratitude to Daniel Cumerlato and Stephanie Lechniak, who generously spent many hours sharing fascinating tales of Hamilton's history and ghosts with me.

I am also indebted to the wonderful staff of the Terryberry and Central Branches of the Hamilton Public Library, who were extremely supportive and helpful in aiding me in my research needs; in particular, Laura Lamb, Margaret Houghton, and Robert Oldham.

I would also like to thank all of the good folks at Dundurn who had a hand in producing this book, especially Beth Bruder for believing in the project from the beginning, Michael Carroll and Shannon Whibbs for the ongoing support, and my editor, Matt Baker, for polishing, guidance, and endless patience.

And, as always, my gratitude goes out to Francine and Alexander, who forgave my repeated absences while I was doing research or had sequestered myself in the den for countless hours, working on this book.

INTRODUCTION

I've always been afraid of the monster under my bed, of the ever-growing shadows that begin to stretch and creep across the room, ever-larger as the sun begins its descent in the western sky. Ever since I was a young boy, I've darted up the basement stairs, just in case the creature that lives behind the furnace decides to come out and get me, and I've closed the closet door that final crack so the ghost that lives inside can't get out.

One of my favourite things about being a Cub Scout was going on the camping trips and listening to ghost stories in front of the fire well into the wee hours of the morning. I was held in rapt fascination, getting a chill from hearing "true tales" shared by fellow scouts and scout leaders. Sleep deprivation was simply an added benefit: the less sleep you got, the more your mind began to create monsters out of the shadows and turn every strange noise into some sort of otherworldly creature or horrifying night stalker.

Despite how those nights of stories held my interest, history lessons never really captured my heart or my imagination. Perhaps it had something to do with the manner it was being taught to me; or maybe my young mind was simply closed to how something occurring in the past could be interesting or relevant to me in the present.

Nonetheless, it was about eight years ago that my love for ghost stories and my previous aversion to history collided, offering me a wonderfully serendipitous moment of revelation. My wife Francine and I were back in Ottawa, visiting old friends and some of our favourite haunts (we had moved to Hamilton in 1997 but had met in Ottawa, where I'd lived since 1988 when I moved there to attend Carleton University). After a wonderful dinner at D'Arcy McGee's on Sparks Street, just outside the pub we joined a "Haunted Walk" group that took us on a tour behind Parliament Hill, along the Rideau Canal, and into a few neighbourhoods downtown.

It was a late summer evening, but there was a brisk chill in the air. Our group, wearing sweaters and thin fall jackets, huddled around the tour guide — dressed in a dark, flowing robe and carrying a lantern — as we slowly moved on a short pilgrimage through time. During the walk, we learned a great deal about the history of the many buildings, of the construction of the canal, and, of course, of the accompanying ghost stories.

Learning about the history, and how it affected the ghostly tales and legends associated with various locations, was just the kick-start my imagination needed to absorb and appreciate Canada's past. My previous aversion to historic tales was shed, and I listened with bated breath to the tour guide as the stories of the history and local legends of ghosts rolled off her tongue.

During the tour, I felt shivers crawling up and down my spine, but I also marvelled at the tales of people who had walked the very same ground decades or even hundreds of years before me — people whose spirits seemed to be present with us on our historic walk.

That evening, history came alive for me: it leapt off of the pages of history books and became a real, live, waking thing. My mind finally put together the connection between then and now, and for the first time, I fully appreciated how others could find historical accounts of people, places, and times so absolutely captivating.

Since then, I have been fascinated with ghost walks and with historic walking tours and was thrilled to learn that Hamilton has just such a group. Daniel and Stephanie, founders of Haunted Hamilton Ghost Walks & Events, have been offering their special blend of investigative paranormal research and historical preservation for over ten years. Their company offers several local ghost walks and historic tours, a ghostly Victorian parlour theatre, and many other themed special events in Hamilton, Niagara-on-the-Lake, and farther outlying destinations.

Over the years, I have not only enjoyed the offerings that Daniel, Stephanie, and their magnificent team bring to the Hamilton region, but I have also worked with them, creating a Haunted McMaster evening in late October, which ran in 2008 and 2009. The night featured short custom ghost walks of the McMaster campus, beginning and ending at the bookstore, which hosted horror writers doing readings and signing their books until midnight.

When I started writing this book, it almost went without saying that I would spend time learning as much as I could from Daniel, Stephanie, and their team. Many of the tales that follow are thanks to their generous sharing of time and information.

Some of the marvellous side effects of working on this book were the time I spent talking with people like Daniel and Stephanie, the many books and articles I read, and the time I spent with folks from the Hamilton Public Library, who helped me dig into various archives and historic scrapbooks to find more information about places and people from Hamilton's past.

With almost every item I uncovered, I was tempted to keep exploring, keep digging for more. I found myself having to pull back on several occasions and withdraw from the rich historic detail I was poring through. For that reason, I have included a long list of suggested readings at the end of this book. These represent a selection of the many talented, passionate writers who have pooled their resources together to share what makes Hamilton a dynamic and significant city, both historically and in modern terms.

Upon digging through documents, listening to first-person accounts, and looking at pictures, I found the need to stand in the very spots I was writing about and experience the subtle ripples of history crossing my psyche.

Perhaps it is not surprising, then, that through the course of writing this book — in both the research as well as the visits to haunted landmarks — I scared myself silly. One might expect that from a man who readily admits he is still cautious about the monster under the bed, but even in the re-writing and editing of the very stories you're about to see, I experienced that wonderfully creepy spine-tingling sensation.

And that's why I am delighted with the opportunity to put together a book that combines two things I am quite passionate about. Hopefully, I can share a little bit of the "thrill-seeker" in me who enjoys a chilling true ghost story, as well as my newly discovered appreciation of a fascinating and rich history.

So, if you're ready, turn the lights down, get comfortable, and join me on an enriching journey of historic fact merged with local legend and lore. And if you think you hear something, or detect a subtle shift in the shadows, don't worry: it's just your imagination putting in a little overtime.

Or is it?

CHAPTER ONE

THE CUSTOM HOUSE

The most famous Hamilton ghost, and one who is thought to inhabit the Custom House, is likely the Dark Lady, or "The Black Lady," from an 1873 poem by Alexander Hamilton Wingfield:

> A "Peeler," who met her, turned blue with affright,
> And in terror he clung to a post;
> His hair (once a carroty red) has turned white,
> Since the moment he looked on the ghost.[1]

A Designated National Historic Site, the Hamilton Custom House was built from 1858 to 1860 in a design by Frederick J. Rastrick and F.P. Rubridge. The building is a fine example of Italianate architecture, which was popular in commercial buildings between the 1840s and 1870s in Canada. The rusticated base and smooth upper storey drew inspiration from Renaissance-style palaces in Florence and Rome.[2]

One of the oldest remaining formerly federal buildings in Canada, the Custom House is regularly cited as one of Hamilton's foremost architectural landmarks. The history of the building is varied, but it began as a location where officials handled the paperwork for all goods leaving and entering the city. The many different uses, owners, and businesses of the building add to the richness of its history — as well as the speculation that more than one spirit haunts the century-and-a-half old building. Apart from the Dark Lady, definitely the most reported ghost of the Custom House, it is rumoured that as many as twenty-five spectres roam the halls of this building.

In 1855 construction of the Custom House was authorized, to handle the trade flowing through the new Great Western Railway and the Port of Hamilton. Upon the building's completion in 1860, a group of seventeen men worked there as Customs Department staff, dealing with railwaymen, teamsters, and sailors. The caretaker of the Custom House and his family lived on the premises.[3]

In 1887 the Customs Department moved to what was the old post office building — a bigger office — at the corner of King and John Streets in downtown Hamilton. That same year, the Hamilton Board of Education rented the Custom House, setting up classes and a playground. At this time, the janitor of the Murray Street School, located behind the Custom House, was given a place to live in the building. He and his family remained residents there for two decades.[4]

In 1893 the Hamilton YWCA rented the building, offering women classes in sewing, cooking, and housekeeping; this lasted for approximately one year before it relocated to the former Hamilton Street Railway offices.[5]

In 1908 the Associated Charities of Hamilton took over the building, providing accommodations for the homeless and recent immigrants. It wasn't uncommon for hobos who were riding the rails to spend the night in the basement of the Custom House.[6]

By 1912 the Custom House stood empty, barren, and derelict, with broken windows, torn-out pipes, and a leaking roof. Owners of a nearby vinegar factory temporarily moved

Courtesy of Peter Rainford.

The Hamilton Custom House is an excellent example of Italianate architecture in Canada.

their operations into the building when a fire destroyed their own. In 1915 the Woodhouse Invigorator Company and the American Computing Company rented spaces in the building for manufacturing of their products. In 1917 the Ontario Yarn Company (later known as the Empire Wool Stock Company) moved in.[7]

A devastating fire broke out in 1920, destroying the second floor and roof. The ruined upper configuration of the building was rebuilt, and the second floor, which had originally boasted extremely high ceilings, was reconfigured into two floors and an attic.[8]

The Empire Wool Stock Company, which took residence for longer than any of the previous occupants, beginning at a time when Hamilton's nickname might have easily been "Textile Town" rather than "Steel City," closed down in the 1950s. This was a period of transition, and many Hamilton textile mills and knitwear plants also closed as the city became increasingly dependent on steel and related industries.[9]

The Naples Macaroni Company, producing macaroni and olives, opened in the building in 1956 and holds the record as the second-longest occupant. It also rented space on the first floor to a manufacturer of doughnuts. It was during this era that bugs and rats began to invade the building, and the owners heavily sprayed it with pesticides. In their haste to rid the building of its uninvited guests, they inadvertently contaminated the food, which eventually resulted in the Health Department closing them down in 1979.[10]

The building again sat empty and decaying, subject to damage from neglect and vandals, until 1988, when the provincial government invested $400,000 into restorations. The renovated structure was then inhabited by a martial arts academy and a computer company until the Ontario Workers' Art and Heritage Centre (WAHC) bought it in 1995 with the goal of creating a museum celebrating the working-class people of Canada. The WAHC held a one-day pre-renovation opening to celebrate the long history of the building and in 1996 reopened it as an interpretive centre for workers' history and culture.[11]

Indeed, while the building has a rich history involving workers and their culture, it is also steeped in the richness of spirits that allegedly haunt it.

As mentioned, the most famous is the Dark Lady, who is often described as a pretty woman with dark hair — usually tied back in a bun — and wearing a dark dress. She has been spotted brushing her long black hair in front of a vintage mantelpiece and is known to be very protective of the building when any changes are made to it.

Apparently, a painter who was working there received an eerie message from the Dark Lady. She informed him that if her mantelpiece was moved, as was planned for a renovation, the building and the worker would be "washed away." The painter relayed the message to management, but the mantle was moved anyway. And the next day, a drain pipe burst, causing some water damage.

There is another legend of a different painter working in the front hallway. He was startled to see the word MURDER appear in the freshly rolled paint, as if written with someone's finger — only the words were backwards, as though being written from the other side of the wall.

Stephanie Lechniak, co-founder of Haunted Hamilton Ghost Walks & Events, has expressed a particular affinity with the Custom House building. When she was a child, her father used to bring her to look at the beautiful architecture of the building, and these days the Custom House is a big part of the ghost walks and costume ball put on by Haunted Hamilton.

Stephanie tells the tale of a Halloween in 2005 when she may have personally witnessed the Dark Lady. Sitting at the front of the main gallery, scraping a bit of wax from one of the tables, Stephanie heard a quiet creaking emanating from the old wood floors. Familiar with the building's history and the spirits, particularly the Dark Lady, she steeled her nerves before looking up.

She saw a young woman sitting in a chair directly in front of her. The woman was there for just a moment before disappearing.

"The Dark Lady," Lechniak notes, "is said to be the spirit of an unfortunate young Englishwoman who had gotten herself pregnant and was subsequently shunned in her home country and sent by ship to Canada to start a new life with her baby."[12]

On the overseas voyage, the woman apparently had an affair with the ship's captain. The captain, who had intended for the encounter to be a mere fling, was repulsed by the neediness of this woman. Her desire for them to stay together and for him to be the father of her child horrified him in terms of what it would mean for his reputation.

It is rumoured that, during a heated argument on the ship's deck, the captain killed her in a fit of rage, snuck her body into the Custom House, and bricked it up behind a basement wall.

The Custom House does have a superfluous wall in the basement, but the historic designation has prevented any investigators from breaking it down to see if there is indeed evidence of a body and a crime. For most people, though, the brick wall's existence and the tales that permeate the building are evidence enough.

Other ghosts haunting the building include those of two little boys, who have been heard running on the second floor by employees of the main floor's gift shop. Another is that of a young woman, raped and killed in the building, who is said to be buried out back. Her spirit is believed to haunt the stairs inside and has been seen sitting forlornly on the stairway.

Additional lost souls include those of the fifteen men who were buried alive when the tunnel between the house and the railway tracks collapsed on them. Because they were transients, nobody knew who they were or even if there were families to be notified. The tunnel was simply sealed up, and everyone pretended that nothing had happened. As Daniel Cumerlato of Haunted Hamilton put it, "If you look in the basement, you can plainly see where the tunnel has been sealed, forever trapping those inside. With no proper burial or funerary rites, who could be surprised that these souls remain trapped in the world of the living?"[13] With so many dead buried in and around the Custom House, it's no wonder there are ongoing tales of people witnessing the supernatural.

A fitting end to this chapter on the Custom House might very well be the origin to the legends set in this historic building — a poem written by the Custom House employee Alexander Hamilton Wingfield, published in 1873.

The Woman in Black

The ghosts — long ago — used to dress in pure white,
Now they're got on a different track, —

For the Hamilton Ghost seems to take a delight
To stroll 'round the city in black.

Pat Duffy, who saw her in Corktown last night,
Has been heard to-day telling his friend
That she stood seven feet and nine inches in
height,
And wore a large Grecian Bend.

A "Peeler,"* who met her, turned blue with affright,
And in terror he clung to a post;
His hair (once a carroty red) has turned white,
Since the moment he looked on the ghost.

Her appearance was frightful to gaze on, he
said, —
It filled him with horror complete;
For she looked unlike anything, living or dead,
That ever he'd seen on his beat.

Her breath seemed as hot as a furnace; besides, —
It smelt strongly of sulphur and gin,
Two horns (a yard long) stuck straight out of
her head,
And her hoofs made great clatter and din.

Her air was majestic, and terribly grand,
As she passed, muffled up in her veil;
A bottle of "ruin" she held in each hand,
And she uttered a low, plaintive wail;

---

* *Peeler* is a historic term that means "police officer." It comes from
Sir Robert Peel, who helped create the modern concept of the police
force. The term *Bobbies* was also derived from his name.[15]

"'There is rest for the weary,'" but no rest for me;
I cannot find rest if I try, —
Three months and three days I have been on
the spree
(Mr. Mueller, 'How's that for high?')

"I have mixed in the world, both with 'spirits'
and men, —
Once more with the spirits I'll go."
She stopped, took a sniff of the "ruin," and then
She popped into a cellar below.

He could hear her again, crying out from her
den —
"To-night you will see me no more;
But I'll meet with you Saturday evening at ten,
By the fountain that stands in the Gore."

Some people that passed there this morning
at two
Found the "Peeler" still glued to his post;
He told them this yarn I have been telling you —
And that's the last news from the Ghost![14]

CHAPTER TWO

THE GHOSTS OF DUNDURN CASTLE

A renowned and much-discussed figure of Canadian history, Sir Allan MacNab was a confident and charismatic man. Even at the age of twenty-eight, he was said to be a man to follow and watch.[1] With societal eyes cast upon him from such an early age through the height of his career in politics and as an important entrepreneurial figure in Hamilton's history, it is no wonder people are fascinated with his home.

The building and estate MacNab left behind, as was the intention from their inception, inspire awe. Set atop a gorgeous series of fields, gardens, forests, and rolling grassy hills, against a stunning backdrop of Lake Ontario, the Dundurn Castle estate is as fascinating as it is beautiful. The grounds and adjacent Dundurn Park are home to receptions, weddings, and corporate events; it has even hosted royal visits, such as that of Charles, the Prince of Wales, and Camilla, the Duchess of Cornwall, in 2009.

But when the sun goes down, the shadows creep and spread, giving the Regency-style villa an entirely different look and feel. With the grounds lit by a full moon hanging low in the sky, just to the side of the pillars of the castle, one begins to ponder the many mysteries and tales surrounding Dundurn Castle.

T. Melville Bailey, a local historian, wrote in 1943 that the tales of secret tunnels extending from Dundurn Castle across the grounds were as old as the castle itself. "But," he notes, "like the ghosts that sit in the castle when the moon is high — we have no positive proof of their existence."[2]

A lack of physical proof, however, doesn't stop the mind from racing or the heart from skipping a beat when experiencing something at Dundurn Castle that defies explanation.

Looking back upon the history of the building, its occupants, and the many alleged occurrences on the grounds and adjacent to the property over the past two centuries helps to cast a light into those dark corners, but perhaps doesn't fully satisfy the mind. The rich history of Dundurn Castle leads to more speculation, further enigmas, and even more possibilities that it is indeed haunted and by more than one ghost.

Dundurn Castle is one of Hamilton's most easily recognized landmarks. A National Historic Site, it was designed by Robert Wetherall, an English architect, and built around the brick shell of Colonel Richard Beasley's colonial home. Often considered Wetherall's masterpiece, it was constructed over a three-year period and completed in 1835.[3]

The gardens, grounds, and many unique and unusual buildings made Dundurn one of the finest estates in the province at that time. *Dundurn* is Gaelic for "strong fort" and the residents of Hamilton immediately nicknamed it "castle."[4]

Sitting high over Burlington Bay, and seen as people enter or exit Hamilton via York Road, Robert Wetherell meant for this stunning Italianate building to be viewed from the water. The goal was to design and build a house that would not only demonstrate Sir Allan MacNab's wealth and importance but also to make a mark on the colonial society, both in his day and in the years that followed.[5]

MacNab's house was "a statement of an age that was already passing"[6] — one in which eighteenth-century aristocrats designed,

Courtesy of Peter Rainford.

Dundurn Castle is a historic neoclassical mansion that was completed in 1835. It is 18,000 square feet (1,700 square metres) and took three years and $175,000 to build.

constructed, landscaped, and furnished homes that conveyed their families' prestige to the community. Similar to the newest homes in Britain at the time, Dundurn was designed to be looked upon as well as to look outward (particularly across the bay). The ground-floor windows could be swung open and stepped through for easy access to the manicured lawns.

The home itself was relatively narrow, considering that the building was constructed on top of Richard Beasley's earlier home (he was a fur trader and one of Hamilton's first residents). This was an intentional statement by MacNab, implying that the future was firmest when built upon the past, and it affected the layout of the interior of the home — something that is not evident when looking upon the building from outside.[7]

Today, Dundurn has been restored to the year 1855, when Sir Allan Napier MacNab (1798–1862) was at the height of his career as a lawyer, land owner, railway magnate, and premier of the "United Canadas." More than forty rooms of the seventy-two-room castle have been furnished, and costumed staff guide visitors through the home, richly illustrating the life of a prominent Victorian family and contrasting it with that of their servants.[8]

MacNab was born in Niagara-on-the-Lake and arrived in Hamilton from York in 1826, beginning his career as a lawyer. That same year he lost his first wife, Elizabeth Brookes, and raised his two children, Robert and Anne Jane, as a widower. In 1831 he married Mary Stuart and had two more children, Sophia and Minnie. During the construction of Dundurn, in 1934, MacNab's son Robert fatally shot himself in a hunting accident on the grounds of Dundurn.[9] Later, in 1846, Mary died of consumption. Outside of her deathbed room, a cool chill and mysterious breeze that blows out candles continues to mystify visitors and staff.

According to the tour guides at Haunted Hamilton, an employee of the castle who was performing a last-minute check before locking up one night encountered an eerie sensation in Mary's bedroom. Alone in the room, she was surprised to hear something: "I was putting out a candle when I heard the sound of a singing voice. At first I thought: *Oh, doesn't that sound nice.*" But then she wondered what it was and where she could be hearing singing from. After all, there was no radio playing, nobody around, and the sound definitely wasn't coming from outside. "It wasn't frightening," she said, "but it was not explainable. It was just a couple of phrases of singing and it took me by surprise."[10]

In 2000, *Hamilton Spectator* reporter Paul Wilson wrote about the 1999 wedding of Carol and Jim Forrest. Shortly after their ceremony, Carol, Jim, and the wedding party went to the grounds of Dundurn Castle to have their wedding pictures — hundreds — taken professionally. When the photos were delivered a couple of weeks later, Carol and Jim weren't sure what to make of one in particular: visible immediately behind Lloyd, Carol's brother, is a pale, grey face.

Attempting to investigate the mysterious wedding guest, Carol took the photograph to various photo shops, Dundurn, an occult store, and a Caledonia psychic. The psychic told Carol the name of the extra guest was Sophia, who felt such spiritual energy and comfortable to be overseeing the wedding.[11] Local historian T. Melville Bailey reported that a Sophia was married in Dundurn in November of 1855, moved with her husband to England, and lived the rest of her life there in luxury, never returning to North America.

Of course, there are those who speculate that spirits don't necessarily have to haunt the place where they died and can linger behind or return to visit a place that held importance to them in life. So there is the possibility that Sophia, who was married in the castle, returns as a spectral guest to look upon weddings and bestow a positive omen on the festivities.

Apart from his many prestigious roles, MacNab was also a carpenter, stage actor, military officer, and baron. Eclectic in his ways, he was sometimes seen as a man of dual personalities. He displayed an intense degree of power and wealth yet died almost without a penny in his pocket. He was seen as a compassionate and kind employer to his servants yet was a ruthless and threatening businessman.

It has been said that one of Sir Allan MacNab's hobbies was playing the bagpipes; not just inside the home for his family but also sometimes outside in the middle of the night — on the roof. One can imagine the haunting droning of the bagpipes in the thick dark of night, echoing off the moonlit structures and nearby cemetery tombstones.

In many historical accounts, MacNab is often overshadowed by contemporaries such as John A. Macdonald, even though he played a significant role in laying the foundations for the industrial growth in Hamilton as well as for prosperity in much of Southern Ontario.

MacNab died on August 8, 1862, at Dundurn Castle.[12] He was originally buried that same year on the Dundurn Park grounds between Dundurn Castle and what is known as Castle Dean, on the corner of Locke and Tecumseh.[13] In 1909 MacNab's body was removed and taken to Holy Sepulchre Cemetery in West Hamilton. His grave was left unmarked until 1967, when the Canadian Club of Hamilton placed a bench and grave marker there.

Due to the huge amount of debt that MacNab died with, the property was mortgaged to pay off his creditors, and the castle sat empty for several years before becoming an institution for the deaf in 1866. It was then purchased in 1872 by Donald McInnes, who moved his family in after making some minor revisions and repairs to the estate.[14]

In 1899 McInnes sold the castle to the City of Hamilton and it became a museum. In 1967, for the Canadian Centennial year, three million dollars was spent restoring the castle to the state it was in when Sir Allan MacNab inhabited it.[15]

Constructed of stone, a "mystery building," with a small pagoda-like upper level and topped with a circular cap and column, exists at Dundurn Park, just east of the castle. Nobody knows the actual purpose for which it was built, but historians feel that it might have been a boathouse, an office, a theatre, a laundry, a summer pavilion, or a chapel. Urban legends posit that many underground tunnels lead from the castle to other buildings on the estate, one of them coming through this mystery building.[16, 17]

The site itself, even prior to the castle being constructed, is not immune to the possibility of ghosts. Many Hamilton residents stricken with cholera during their passage overseas were housed in — and died in — plague sheds across the street from where the castle now stands. And in 1812, eleven men (American sympathizers during the war) were publicly gutted and hung for treason.

All of this aside — staff and visitors alike feeling cold chills, witnessing apparitions gliding through rooms of the castle and in the moonlight yard, reporting various objects being moved around — the castle and its grounds continue to exude a sense of enigma and mystery.

And if you visit Dundurn today, you'll see that it stands, like its original owner, not just as a beacon of a significant time in Hamilton history but also as an acknowledgement that some of our most interesting pieces of history remain unsolved puzzles.

CHAPTER THREE

BELLEVUE MANSION

When I first moved to Hamilton in 1997, my wife took me down a street on the edge of the Niagara Escarpment, pointing out an old house that had been abandoned since she was a child. She talked about that common childhood experience regarding old, creepy abandoned houses: almost every town or neighbourhood has one. One that children regularly cast leery glances at and step a bit more quickly when passing the sidewalk in front, particularly when the sun begins to set and the shadows grow long.

The neighbourhood and lot were actually desirable, and as the years passed and the old abandoned building was torn down, Francine and I speculated that it would be a great property to purchase and build a house on. It is a decent-sized lot on a lovely street, close to the amenities we're used to and near the school our son attends. And the view of the city was spectacular.

We made some basic inquiries regarding the property, but nobody ever got back to us. I thought it was strange that a salesperson wouldn't respond to a call from a serious customer. It was only later that I discovered some of the history of that lot and its "haunted house" — and was glad that a salesperson never returned my calls.

Francine and I now merely need to mention that abandoned lot and a shared chill runs up our spines.

The stories we have heard cause the imagination to run wild, conjuring haunting visions of a deranged man, a domestic predator, slowly lumbering through the halls in search of his family. In these thoughts, the house, the very grounds themselves, are possessed of some evil spirits that could drive a man to commit unspeakable acts.

But I have gotten ahead of myself here. Let's go back to look at the house in question and learn a bit about its history.

The Bellevue Mansion stood atop the mountain brow for over 150 years[1] with a commanding view out over the city and bay. It ranked among Hamilton's finest examples of historic residential architecture. Built by John Bradley between 1848 and 1850 of local quarried limestone, the Bellevue Mansion (*bellevue* being a French term for "beautiful view") closely resembled the McQuesten homestead of Whitehern, both in style and construction.[2] Of particular significance are the north, east, and west facades, the stone chimneys, and belvedere of the building.[3]

The symmetrical and compact Classical Revival design of Bellevue displayed the finest sense of scale and proportion from the beginning, a testament to the competence of builders Melville, Herald, and White. Later embellished with a belvedere (after which the street is named), the Bellevue was one of the first in Hamilton's tradition of beautiful escarpment estates.[4]

In the nineteenth century, Bellevue — along with other contemporary limestone mansions such as Inglewood, Rock Castle, and Whitehern — marked an important initial step in Hamilton's rapid transition from a pioneer settlement to a cosmopolitan centre.[5]

The original owner of Bellevue, John Bradley, contributed to the Hamilton region not only through his commercial success (he owned a tavern, two downtown hotels, and land in the Hamilton area) but also through his political leadership in the growth of the community. Mr. Bradley, who had Bellevue built to accommodate him in his retirement, was a lieutenant, a major in the militia, and was appointed to the Board of Police. He is also often known as the man responsible for bringing the Roman Catholic Church to Hamilton. He retired a wealthy man and lived a good life until he died in the home in 1864.[6]

In the 1860s and 1870s George Gillespie, a later resident of 14 Belvidere, was a successful merchant and industrialist who did many things to promote Hamilton financial institutions.[7]

In the years since then, many other people lived in the residence, often home to distinguished citizens such as the Innes family, who took it over in the 1930s. Conversely, just as it was known to be the home of upstanding citizens, it was also rumoured to be the setting for some lurid and horrific occurrences.

It is said that a loving family — happy, comfortable, and content — once lived in the house, until one night, under the light of a full moon, the father stalked quietly up and down the hallways, wordlessly sinking an axe into the flesh of his two children and his wife. Upon completion of this gruesome task, legend has it that he climbed upstairs to the widow's walk, where he hung himself from the main wooden beam of the belvedere.

The next morning, the police found the family butchered in their beds and the father's body swaying in the attic. As evidenced by the tale of another family that lived there, the deceased may have been victims of some evil spirit that possessed the father.

This second story involves a son who, like the previous tenant, found an axe — perhaps the very same axe used in the first murders — and, again under a full moon, killed his family before taking his own life with that worn out beam on the widow's walk.

Of course, frightening rumours like this spread like wildfire in the midst of a dry summer, passed not only from child to child but adult to adult. In the presence of such shameless decay, it's no wonder that people cling to bizarre tales without any evidence. It's as if believing something supernatural is taking place provides justification for the building going unlived-in for so long.

The lot at 14 Belvdere Avenue now stands empty. The house, as captured in this 1999 photo, is but a memory that will haunt Hamilton forever.

Initial searches into whether or not murders actually occurred in this neighbourhood in that time period were inconclusive: no immediate evidence could be found. Claire Sellens purchased the home in 1971, but he never moved in. Instead, he rented it out. As time passed, and the building continued to deteriorate, it was eventually abandoned.[8] It became the house at the end of the street, the one that children, such as my wife and her friends, feared; it became that haunted house, the building with eyes, the one that gave you the creepiest feeling when you walked past it.

Daniel and Stephanie shared a story told to them by a friend of Haunted Hamilton. It happened to a woman close to him one Halloween. Changing her name to Mary, here is how they tell the tale:

> Mary, her boyfriend, and another couple went
> to the Bellevue Mansion at night to explore the
> spooky old house, but also prove for themselves

if the violent ghosts of the murderous man and young boy really did exist.

With them they brought a Ouija board. This was the best way to communicate, as none in the group claimed to have any psychic ability.

They arrived at about 11:00 p.m. that night and spent perhaps an hour walking through the house and looking at all the old rooms.

Mary was disgusted by how decayed the house was, seeing that many of the rooms were damp, mouldy, and some areas were already well beyond repair, including a back room with a caved-in ceiling.

Finally, they set up the Ouija board in the old parlour. Each of the four kids put two fingers on the planchette. Mary's boyfriend called out, summoning the ghosts of the husband and the boy. Time passed and nothing happened.

Just as they were about to give up, Mary heard a knocking from the second floor. The knocking got louder and harder, so much that the house itself started to shake. All four got to their feet and ran for the door, but Mary tripped.

She thought it was just a rock, or something left on the floor, but realized she was wrong when an invisible hand started dragging her back into the house.

Mary's boyfriend saw her being pulled away, but his fear was stronger than his sense of chivalry, and he kept running ... all the way home.

The next day, all the kids met at school, including Mary. She refused to tell any of them what happened after being dragged into the house. But needless to say, Mary and her boyfriend didn't remain a couple after that unique harrowing experience.[9]

Haunted Hamilton also heard from a woman that there was a spirit sighting by a clairvoyant who was visiting the house. The clairvoyant lady, who was standing outside, looked up to see a woman with blazing red hair running back and forth on the second floor, waving her arms frantically in the air.[10]

The clairvoyant also reported seeing the ghostly figure of a man with light brown hair walking toward them on the grounds of the property.

Other common legends and reported paranormal activity occurring at 14 Belvidere include visions of a young girl playing in the front yard and phantom voices whispering out people's names.

Bellevue Mansion, which was popular talk among the local teenagers for rumours of murders, suicides, and ghosts or demons haunting the abandoned lot and building, was Haunted Hamilton's first official investigation, the one that Daniel and Stephanie used as their debut.

They visited the historic house, which they referred to at the time as "Belvidere Mansion," on a beautiful sunny day, taking dozens of pictures with their 35mm Canon camera.

They captured amazing views of extremely high ceilings and walls painted in bright colours, beautiful decorative white plaster mouldings, and large windows that went right up to the ceiling. They witnessed extraordinary views of the city of Hamilton.

But they also caught images of severely water-damaged rooms and a sadly neglected home in a crumbling state of decay. They saw what was once a majestic building of comfort and luxury instead as a barren and deserted shell, echoing with the rumours of murder and evil spirits.

Because it was a popular hangout for thrill-seeking teens and the police were regularly called to visit the home due to the noise, owner Claire Sellens had the support he needed to demolish the building, something that had been opposed by people like Janice Kay and The Committee to Save Bellevue.[11]

Claire Sellens was quoted in the *Hamilton Spectator* as saying, "There comes a time when granny no longer should be maintained on life support."[12] In the fall of 2000, Hamilton lost yet another battle to save a historic building from destruction. Bellevue Mansion was torn down on that fateful day in September.

On an overcast day in early August 2011, I diverted from the path I usually jogged in order to pay yet another visit to this lot that so intrigued my wife and I. Having read so much and written about the history of the building, I simply wanted to visit it one more time and perhaps see if I might sense any of the alleged spectres or even an eerie feeling from being there.

Taking a short pause from my run, I took off my headphones and explored the lot. Then, I hit the record button of the voice memo application on my phone and recorded the following:

> I'm standing in the barren lot where the house used to stand with sheets of misty rain running down and cooling me off from the run I just completed. Three, perhaps four building towers from the city below peek out over the overgrown grass and bushes growing behind the wrought-iron fence at the back of the lot. There are sounds of traffic on the mountain access a hundred feet below. Standing on the spot where the house once stood and looking out onto Belvidere, I can see the entrance to the lot is overgrown with bushy trees and shrubs. I can hear a couple of cars passing by on that front street and catch a quick glimpse of them as they pass a small cut-out window in the canopy of greenery that blocks almost all

of the street from view. This giant, beautiful, overgrown lot has sat vacant now for more than ten years. There's barely any evidence left of the building that once stood here, except perhaps for the eerie feeling that I bring with me from the things I have read about it.

As I stood there recording my thoughts and observations about the lot, I realized that, though I had been prepared to be frightened, though I had been prepared to feel some supernatural chill in the air, perhaps even to sense an evil presence lurking in wait for me, I instead felt sad for the loss our city faced when the building came down.

A barren and overgrown lot stands, still empty, where the Bellevue used to majestically look out over the city from atop the mountain brow for over 150 years. The lot has remained empty since the remains of the building were taken away that fateful September in 2000, and nobody knows if anything will ever stand there again; the continued vacancy of the lot is perhaps evidence enough that people still believe the legends about the evil spirits, which might continue to haunt that land.

Chapter Four

BATTLEFIELD HOUSE MUSEUM

Battlefield House is a living history museum that sits within Battlefield Park, thirty-two acres of field and forest nestled at the foot of the Niagara Escarpment in Stoney Creek near King Street West and Centennial Parkway. The park is the site of the historic Battle of Stoney Creek, which took place on June 6, 1813, during the War of 1812.

In 1812 the United States declared war on Britain and invaded Upper Canada from the border of the Niagara Peninsula. American forces crossed the Niagara River and captured Fort George in Niagara-on-the-Lake (then Newark) in May 1813. Approximately 3,500 American troops moved on in pursuit of the British who had retreated to Burlington Heights, a location in Hamilton where Dundurn Castle now stands.[1]

Approximately three thousand American troops arrived at Stoney Creek on June 5, 1813, and camped down for the night. The Gage House was used as headquarters by the two American generals, William H. Winder and John Chandler.

Early the next morning, the British launched a surprise assault under the cover of darkness. It was made possible through the assistance of Billy Green, a nineteen-year-old local civilian.

Having witnessed the attack from the Niagara Escarpment, Billy rode and walked to Burlington Heights to alert the British soldiers. The British decided on a night attack, and Billy, an experienced woodsman who knew the area well, was given a sword and uniform and acted as a scout.

About seven hundred regulars of the 8th and 49th Regiments of Foot, under Lieutenant-Colonel John Harvey, stopped the American advance and allowed the British to re-establish their position in Niagara.

During the forty-minute battle, hundreds of soldiers died and the British captured the two American generals. The Americans retreated to Forty Mile Creek (Grimsby) and then to Fort George.[2]

This was the last time American soldiers ever advanced so far into the Niagara Peninsula region.

Battlefield Park's tall trees, huge stretches of open space, and winding stream are open for the public to enjoy through each season of the year, with all visitors enjoying and appreciating the natural beauty of the park.

But the ghosts of both the British and American soldiers who died on that very soil are never far from visitors' minds, particularly with the Battlefield Monument — one hundred feet tall and the second-largest monument built in Canada to commemorate the War of 1812 — standing over the grounds.

Influenced by the towering monument to Admiral Nelson at Calton Hill, erected in 1816 in Edinburgh, Scotland, Battlefield Monument is a tapered, castellated tower that rises from a buttressed base. It was designed in the English Gothic Revival style. Observation decks at the top of the base and tower afford picturesque views of the entire battlefield.[3]

The monument was constructed shortly after the turn of the century, at a time when men and women were active in improving their communities through the development of schools, libraries, and museums. A small group of citizens formed the Wentworth Historical Society in December of 1888.[4] The women of the group, led by Sara Calder, formed a separate group in 1899 called the Women's Wentworth Historical Society. Through their spirited fundraising, organizing, and work with the federal government, the park was opened to the public and work began on the monument.

In 1900 the architectural firm of F.J. Rastrick and Sons submitted a design for the monument. These plans, in keeping with the nationalistic attitude, called for only Canadian materials such as Queenston limestone to be used.[5]

On the centennial of the Battle of Stoney Creek, June 6, 1913, the completed monument was unveiled by Queen Mary in London, via a transatlantic cable. Approximately fifteen thousand people, both civilians and military, were in attendance, and children were given a half-day off school.[6]

The dedication stone at the base of the monument reads:

UNVEILED BY ELECTRICITY JUNE 6TH 1913 BY

HER MAJESTY QUEEN MARY

THIS MONUMENT WAS ERECTED BY THE PEOPLE OF CANADA, COLONEL THE HONOURABLE SAM HUGHES BEING MINISTER OF MILITIA AND DEFENCE, TO COMMEMORATE THE BATTLE OF STONEY CREEK JUNE 6TH 1813.

THE BRITISH TROOPS UNDER COMMAND OF GENERAL VINCENT AND LIEUT. COLONEL HARVEY CONSISTED OF THE 49TH REG'T IN COMMAND OF MAJOR PLENDERLEATH AND FIVE COMPANIES OF THE 8TH OF KING'S IN COMMAND OF MAJOR OGILVIE, TO WHICH WAS ADDED THE VOLUNTEER ASSISTANCE OF THE SETTLERS HEREABOUTS LED BY CAPT. W.H.MERRITT OF THE CANADIAN MILITIA, THE TOTAL NUMBER BEING ABOUT SEVEN HUNDRED. THE AMERICAN FORCE NUMBERED UPWARDS OF THREE THOUSAND UNDER COMMAND OF GENERALS CHANDLER AND WINDER.

THEY WERE ENCAMPED IN THIS IMMEDIATE VICINITY WITH STAFF HEADQUARTERS IN THE GAGE FARM HOUSE, NOW MAINTAINED BY THE WOMENS WENTWORTH HISTORICAL SOCIETY THROUGH WHOSE REPRESENTATIONS AND UNDER WHOSE DIRECTION THIS MEMORIAL WAS BUILT.

IN THE DEAD OF NIGHT THE BRITISH ADVANCED FROM BURLINGTON HEIGHTS AND SURPRISING THE ENEMY, PUT HIM TO CONFUSION. THIS IS HELD TO HAVE BEEN THE DECISIVE ENGAGEMENT IN THE WAR OF 1812–13.

HERE THE TIDE OF INVASION WAS MET AND TURNED BY THE PIONEER PATRIOTS AND SOLDIERS OF THE KING OF ONE HUNDRED YEARS AGO.

MORE DEADLY THAN THEIR LIVES THEY HELD THOSE PRINCIPLES AND TRADITIONS OF BRITISH LIBERTY OF WHICH CANADA IS THE INHERITOR.[7]

Down the hill from the monument, facing King Street and central to the mystique of this location, lies Battlefield House. It was the homestead of the widow Mary Jones Gage and her two children, James Jr. and Elizabeth. Her husband, James Gage Sr., died in the American Revolutionary War while defending Fort Clinton against the British. Mrs. Gage and her children packed up their belongings, came to the Stoney Creek area in 1790, and received a grant of two hundred acres in exchange for swearing allegiance to the British monarchy.[8]

First built as a rough-hewn log house, the building was replaced in 1796 by a storey-and-a-half frame Georgian-style home, built with symmetrically balanced windows, a steep roof, a huge veranda, and large chimneys.[9]

In 1813 the house was taken over by American soldiers who used it for their headquarters, imprisoning Mrs. Gage and her children in the basement. After the battle, the Gage family eventually returned to their normal lives and James went into business. In 1830 the house was renovated to include a full two storeys. In 1835, Mary Gage moved to Hamilton with her family, selling the farm.[10]

The building exchanged hands many times in the following years, and, like so many historically significant buildings in the Hamilton area, was in a terrible state of repair and in danger of being torn down.

Sara Calder, granddaughter of James and Mary Gage and president of the ladies committee of the Wentworth Historical Society, had the foresight to recognize the historical value of the property. She purchased the house and adjacent four-and-a-half-acre property surrounding it; this property was eventually transferred to the Wentworth Historical Society.[11]

The Wentworth Historical Society restored and refurnished the house to open it as a museum (one of the first museums in Canada), then purchased additional land, built the monument, and opened Battlefield Park.[12]

In 1962, when the Society was unable to keep up the grounds and the house, the Niagara Parks Commission took it over. In the 1970s, the house was restored to its 1835 state.[13]

In 1988 the City of Stoney Creek assumed responsibility for the property,[14] and a group of dedicated volunteers continue to assist staff members with the park and museum's operation. For thirty years now, each June the Battlefield House Museum and Park presents the annual re-enactment of the Battle of Stoney Creek. In 2011 this re-enactment was declared one of the top one hundred events in Ontario by Festivals and Events Ontario. This historic event allows families to experience first-hand the thrill and pageantry of a battle that represented a significant turning point in the War of 1812.[15]

Annually, thousands of people virtually step back in time to visit the encampment, mingle with early nineteenth-century soldiers, and witness historical demonstrations of cooking, blacksmithing, dancing, games, and musical entertainment.[16] But as they move among the white tents, strewn across the field like ghostly reminders of the hundreds of soldiers whose lives were lost on these grounds, they perhaps feel the presence of something else.

Haunted Hamilton has received multiple reports of people witnessing misty soldiers moving silently across the historic battlefield, sometimes with the ghostly echoes of cannons firing in the air.

But, to date, the most fascinating and consistent reports of supernatural activity involve one particular ghost who is said to reside in Battlefield House. Though there are not many claims

Courtesy of Stephanie Lechniak

Battlefield House was originally the homestead of the widow Mary Jones Gage and her children.

of sighting of a physical apparition, many stories are told about the playful and mischievous spirit, thought to be that of Mrs. Gage herself, the home's original owner.

The location of the bodily remains of Mrs. Gage, who died in 1841, remains a mystery, though they were reportedly interred in a lead-lined casket in the First United Church (which burned down in 1969). After this devastating fire, the remains of Mary and other early settlers of the time are said to have been relocated to the Woodland Cemetery in Burlington, where a plaque was erected in their honour.[17] It is further posited that Mary Gage's headstone and body disappeared in the move — and that her restless spirit has found its way back to Battlefield House.

Reports include antique pieces, particularly ones that Mrs. Gage Sr. would have used, disappearing from a room, only to be found in a completely different part of the house several days later. The spirit of Mary is said to be responsible for the occasional electrical malfunction of vacuum cleaners and computers.[18] Additionally, a clairvoyant who toured the house was disturbed by a pervasive aura of violence in one of the front bedrooms. She also experienced what she described as a benevolent spirit with a strong personality.[19]

Over the years, amateurs and seasoned supernatural investigators alike have compiled various audio, video, and photographic materials. The findings range from spectral orbs and eerie shadows appearing in photographs to unexplainable sounds and voices.

One thing that is certain, though, is that any place in which so many lives were lost suddenly and violently is certain to be a hotspot for paranormal activity.

CHAPTER FIVE

THE DEVIL'S PUNCHBOWL

Sometimes referred to as Horseshoe Falls for the distinctive shape of its cliff-face (and somewhat resembling its larger, more well-known cousin in Niagara), the Devil's Punchbowl consists of two separate falls: Upper and Lower Punchbowl Falls. The Upper Falls is a 5.5-metre classic waterfall and the main Lower Falls is a 33.8-metre ribbon waterfall, resulting in one of the Niagara Escarpment's most amazing sights.[1]

The waterfall is part of one of the many "passive areas" maintained by the Hamilton Conservation Authority (HCA). The term *passive* is one that the Conservation Authority itself recognizes the irony in, since there is nothing passive about the more than three thousand hectares of regional passive areas that play a major role in the ecology and health of the region. The term doesn't refer to the landscape itself, but rather to the fact that, though the combined areas annually cost about $1,800 per hectare to maintain, the HCA doesn't charge an admission fee.[2]

The Dofasco 2000 Trail — an 11.5-kilometre trail through upper Stoney Creek that features a long boardwalk section through Vinemount Swamp Forest — begins here, as do several escarpment access trails with connections to the eight-hundred-kilometre-long Bruce Trail.[3]

Although the falls dry up often, rainstorms and melting snow will cause the water to flow, and though flow is typically a thin trickle, it is still an impressive sight, with the water cascading down almost forty metres of free fall.[4]

Widely hailed as one of the region's most impressive sights, the backdrop or horseshoe shape to the waterfall consists of multi-coloured stratified rock layers of the Niagara Escarpment, best visible from the bottom of the falls. The Hamilton Conservation Authority explains that "the Punch Bowl is the only area where one can view such a large vertical display of Ordovician and Silurian stratified rock. Some of the layers include Queenston Formation red shale, Cabot Head grey shale, limestone, and shale dolomite."[5]

The history of the Devil's Punchbowl dates back more than 450 million years, when materials that form the Niagara Escarpment were originally deposited in a large inland sea, which most likely originated from the Appalachian Mountains in the eastern United States. As the sea bottom deposits slowly changed to rock, corals and other organisms became fossilized.[6]

About one million years ago, the area was subjected to several ice ages, with the inland sea retracting and great slabs of ice covering the land. The effect of this ice on the landscape was dramatic; in some places it exposed the escarpment rock face, and in others it buried it farther beneath drifting material.[7]

At the end of the last ice age, a period of high water levels etched and carved many fine details into the landscape of the Niagara and Hamilton region. Powerful runoff streams from the melting ice plunged over the escarpment at Stoney Creek, carving out a gorge that seems almost bottomless if viewed from the safe side of the surrounding guardrail.[8]

Numerous stories circulate as to how the Devil's Punchbowl got its name. One possibility is that it was named for the pails of home brew that, at one time, was bootlegged in the surrounding woods. Rumours abound regarding moonshiners who made their product available along Ridge Road, with thirsty road workers claiming to go to the waterfall to fill their buckets but instead filling up with the devil's brew.

Another story suggests that people saw the beautiful sight as God's work but, knowing that God would not want something named after him, decided they would name it after the devil instead.

And although the Devil's Punchbowl may not have been named after God, one monument located at the site is a large, ten-meter high steel cross, erected by a man named William Sinclair (1925–1994) on December 18, 1966. Sinclair wanted to bring a little light to the world by building the steel monument, which has 106 light bulbs along its edges. It was originally planned to be lit up for six weeks of each year, during Christmas and Easter.[9]

Since 1991, however, the cross has been lit up every night of the year, sharing the "Good will of God" with one and all, thanks to donations made by a Stoney Creek branch of the Knights of Columbus.[10]

An incredible view is offered by the Devil's Punchbowl and the platform erected there. It overlooks Stoney Creek, Hamilton Harbour, and the Skyway Bridge. From the lookout spot, a trail descends down into the gorge. The first half is quite steep and difficult to traverse, but the second half is a stairway that leads to a trail to the creek at the base of the falls.

As with any stunningly picturesque and magnificent historical area, legends abound regarding the Devil's Punchbowl. Despite being an ideal spot for photography or romantic picnics, the site has been the scene of much vandalism. The HCA had to shut down the stone washroom building many years ago due to vandalism, and it's still not uncommon for picnic tables, lengths of fence, and other miscellaneous debris to be tossed into the bottom of the gorge by vandals. Local residents have also often complained of the drunken parties on summer nights down in the Punchbowl ravine that carry on into the wee hours of the morning.

Courtesy of Stephanie Lechniak.

Despite being the perfect spot for photography or a romantic picnic, the Devil's Punchbowl has been the scene of vandalism and suicides, as well as the source of many eerie legends.

And, due to the nocturnal activity in the area, the site has seen its share of deadly accidents and suicides. There is a legend of a boy and his dog who ventured too close to the edge of the gorge, when the hillside gave away and they plunged to their deaths; this tragic and senseless type of accident is one that is regularly reported in newspapers, the bodies of the deceased often being found the next morning by hikers out for a walk. Young men and women feeling they had nothing to live for have leapt to their deaths from the lookout spot, and a man is even alleged to have hung himself from the railway tracks that run near the base of the gorge.

One of the legends told of the Punchbowl is that of a lone still operator who, on dark and moonless nights, can be heard lugging pails of moonshine along Ridge Road, the eerie red glow of his eyes beaming through the dark — a reminder of the "devil's brew" he was offering.

Due to its magnificent scenery, the Punchbowl has been the location for various television and movie shoots. In 1989, television star Super Dave Osborne taped his "atomic yo-yo" stunt here.[11] As he rode inside the hub of a giant yo-yo suspended from a crane, the yo-yo broke free of its tether and rolled off the cliff, plunging into the ravine.[12]

Both the Devil's Punchbowl and the large illuminated cross were featured in the first few scenes of the 2006 horror film *Silent Hill*,[13] which is about a woman's search for her missing daughter within a small, desolate town. It was a fitting sort of movie for such a picturesque yet ominous piece of Hamilton landscape.

CHAPTER SIX

THE HERMITAGE

About three kilometres west of Ancaster and located in the Dundas Valley is a once-large residence that now stands in ruins. Called the Hermitage or the Hermitage Ruins, they are part of the Hermitage and Gatehouse Museum maintained by the Hamilton Conservation Authority. The location is quite popular with hikers and those interested in the paranormal.[1]

I went on a ghost walk run by Haunted Hamilton as part of their Ghost Walks and Historical Tours[2] under a new moon in July of 2011. Of the phases of the moon, a new moon, the time when the moon is not at all visible to the naked eye, is as significant in terms of ritual as a full moon. And for those who are not interested in the effects of lunar phases on supernatural energy and ritual, walking through a forest at night without a radiant orb in the sky can be that much more unsettling.

Just driving out to the location where the tour began, alone in my car and heading down the long and winding Sulphur Springs Road, I began to feel trepidation set in. It felt as if the forests on either side of the road were closing in on me, that beyond the range of my headlights were eyes following my every movement.

When I arrived at the site, a dark and faceless figure in long, flowing black robes, holding a single white candle, stood by the entrance and greeted me, waving me into the parking lot. It was only after I parked the car and walked out near the gathering crowd awaiting the 10:00 p.m. tour that I started to take comfort in the presence of others around me.

Of course, once the tour began, and Ghost Guide George led our group down the path into the rich blackness of the night and relayed the history of the Hermitage to our group, I again felt the eyes of the forest upon me as I delightedly stepped down the path and into a spooky historical journey.

The first building to appear on the now legendary spot was a small and humble home built in 1830 by Reverend George Sheed, Ancaster's first Presbyterian minister, who had a dream of building and ministering his own church. Unfortunately, Sheed died before fully realizing this dream and his funeral took place in the very church he had been building (the 1st St. Andrew's Church on Mineral Springs Road in Ancaster).[3]

Not long after, the property was sold to Colonel Otto Ives, an English officer who had fought in the Greek War of Independence and emigrated to Ancaster in 1833 with his wife and their beautiful young niece.[4]

A servant of Ives, William Black, fell in love with his master's niece. Some accounts of the tale indicate that Black was a coachman as well as a tutor who was asked to assist the niece with speaking and writing English. The niece apparently felt the same way about Black, and thus began a secret and unfulfilled courtship between the two. When Black finally gathered the courage to meet with his boss, and in the gentlemanly and respectful way of the time ask for his niece's hand in marriage, Ives was outraged. The sheer idea of a servant marrying a woman of station was preposterous, and Ives instantly and vehemently rejected the proposal.

Courtesy of Stephanie Lechniak.

The Hermitage, originally built in 1830 by the Reverend George Sheed, now exists as ruins, inspiring visitors with echoes from times long past.

Stunned and an instantly broken man, Black stumbled out of the house. Unable to bear a life without the woman he loved, Black hung himself.

Conflicting reports reveal Black hanging himself either in a stable or by the branches of a nearby willow tree. But as the legend goes, the next morning, Black was founding hanging by Ives, who proceeded to cut the body down. Because, in those days, the body of a person who committed suicide could not be buried on consecrated ground, Ives took Black's body on a cart and buried him at a nearby crossroads of Sulphur Springs Road and what later became known as Lover's Lane (after this very incident).[5]

The ghost of William Black is said to be heard during the night of a full moon, still crying for his lost love. Others have reported seeing his ghost walking the stretch of road near where his body and the cart were buried, wandering aimlessly in his distress and angst, or moving slowly along the grounds of the Hermitage, seeking, in vain, the woman he could not have.

Daniel Cumerlato tells a tale of one eerie moonlit night. At the end of that particular night's tour, he headed back to the ruins to explain to the people still walking around that the security guard would soon be locking the gate to the parking lot. As he moved around the side wall of the Hermitage building, he spotted two people walking toward him. Daniel called out to them to hurry back to the parking lot, but they paid him no heed.

He called out again, and the two moved into the forest.

Concerned for their safety, Daniel ran after them into the woods with his flashlight, mere seconds behind their own entry. But they were nowhere to be found.

Of even more curiosity, Stephanie, who was a few yards back, saw him addressing the people, then chasing after them, but saw nobody other than Daniel on the grounds ... as if they were visible only to him.

One of the tales told regarding the ruins and Black's ghost involves a new park employee, who, upon approaching the ruins, was disturbed to see a body hanging from a tree. Horrified that someone had committed suicide, he stood there, stunned, unable to do anything except watch the body swaying back and forth in the wind. When the figure suddenly vanished, the terrified employee ran as fast as he could off the grounds. It was only later that he learned of the story of William Black.

In a piece of fiction based upon some real experiences, Rob Howard wrote "The Second Ghost," which ran in the *Hamilton Spectator* on Halloween of 2000. In the piece, he shared a fanciful story that he'd been mulling over in his mind for more than two decades.

Howard was hanging out at the site of the ruins with a group of friends after dark on a moonlit night, telling ghost stories, drinking some beers, and engaging in the kind of playful mischief that teenagers are apt to be up to in the days leading up to Halloween. One of the friends, Kenny, who had been planning on playing a prank on the others, decided to leave the group at a certain point, with the excuse of going to get more beer, but would then hide near the gatehouse, making ghostly noises in order to frighten one of their more jumpy friends.

Shortly after Kenny took off on his own, a ghostly moaning noise could be heard from the gatehouse. Laughing and figuring it for a joke, the friends headed over to greet their friend. The moaning transformed suddenly into the distinct words: "Come to me!" When they got to the gatehouse, they saw the padlock had been broken, and, annoyed their friend had engaged in vandalism, yelled out for him to knock it off and that the joke was over.

When they opened the door, they were shocked to find Kenny, barely lit by the dim light of the moon hanging in a noose, his face purple. The friends immediately rushed over and lifted his dangling legs, got him out of the noose and onto the ground.

He was gasping and barely able to speak, and they partially carried him from the grounds and took off in their car. Not much was spoken about that night or what really happened. The friends all went their separate ways, but Kenny and Mickey, who had been going together since Grade 10, ended up getting married.

It wasn't until more than twenty years later, upon bumping into Mickey, that Howard learned the details of what Kenny had really been up to that night and how he'd found himself almost strangled in the noose.

Kenny had apparently forced the gatehouse door open and hid inside, making the noises to scare his friends. When he spotted the noose hanging there, he thought it would be more frightening, a better effect, if his friends saw him standing on a box with his head in the noose.

Pleased with his prank, and hearing the friends calling out for him to knock it off, Kenny stood with his head in the noose and prepared for their frightened arrival.

That's when he saw a dark figure step out of the shadows, heard a voice say that if Kenny took his place in the noose, he could finally rest, and the box was kicked out from under him.

Seconds later, his friends appeared. It was Mickey who felt something nudge her in the dark and heard a loud, sweet female voice say "Go to him!" That's when she rushed forward, the first to assist with getting Kenny down.

Mickey explained to Howard how she understood the ghost who pushed her forward was that of Mary Kathleen, the young woman William Black could not have. Like Black, she too was heartbroken for the rest of her days over the love she would never have.[6]

Howard explained to me that this published tale was just a story that came from "the Muse that floats above us all, occasionally dumping inspiration on our heads," but that it was built upon true teenage experiences, particularly a girlfriend who refused to go any farther than the fence.

Rob's wonderful tale reminds us of something the folks at Haunted Hamilton often express, particularly during their historic tours: most tales are creative and imaginary elements layered on top of a kernel of truth. The theatrical nature of sharing ghost stories brings with it this wonderful sense of combined curiosity, speculation, and fact.

But the spirits haunting this land belong not only to William Black.

In 1853 the property was purchased by George Browne Leith, and in 1855 he built the stately home — which included a large library, drawing room, dining room, and children's room — as a summer villa. Several smaller attendant buildings, such as a carriage house and servants' quarters, were also constructed on the property.[7]

Constructed of Gasport dolomite and limestone, the villa had a hip roof and French windows opening onto a large veranda.[8] Apart from the large, detailed diorama that stands as the centrepiece to the Hermitage and Gatehouse Museum and hints at the sheer magnitude of what once was, the ruins are all that are left of this once magnificent mansion.

That and perhaps yet another soul who could not bear to leave even after her death.

The youngest child of George Leith and his wife Eleanor Ferrier, Alma Dick-Lauder (1854–1942) purchased the property after her mother's death. Alma was a bit of a loner, a writer with a penchant for the preservation of history with a focus on regional landmarks. She wrote articles for the *Hamilton Spectator*, which, ironically, focused on "delving among the ruins," describing graveyards, mills, and churches that had been abandoned by time.[9]

In October 1934, a devastating fire destroyed most of her home. At the age of seventy-nine, she was not about to leave her home, even though very little of the building still stood. She erected a tent to live in the shadow of the standing stone structure. Eventually, a small home was built on that spot, and she remained there until she died in 1942 at the age of eighty-seven.

She had apparently wanted to be buried on the very grounds of the place she so loved, but she was buried in the St. John's Anglican Church cemetery in Ancaster.[10] But that doesn't seem to stop her from returning to the land and building she so cherished in life.

In Alma's book *Pen and Pencil Sketches of Wentworth Landmarks*, published by The Spectator Printing Company, Ltd. in 1897, she writes that one "feels for houses that have known good days and handsome furniture, almost as if they felt their degradation themselves and shivered o' nights in the cold and darkness."[11]

Several times in the book she talks about waking the ghosts of old (of both people and animals), of being in old houses and having "ghosts seem to flit noiselessly"[12] before her, or, more poetically, describing a house as past the stage when even a friendly mouse would run over its old floor — and a ghost there might be, "perhaps in the winter dusk, coming from the radiant fire-lit drawing-room suddenly, a black, shadowless Pompey might be met climbing the stairs with noiseless feet, bearing an impalpable jug of hot water to a massa dead this fifty years and more!"[13]

One legend tells of an engineer, eager to study the remains of the building's foundation, approaching the Hermitage in the middle of a bright day. However, instead of the ruins, he beheld a stately stone mansion drifting in and out of focus like some sort of mirage. As he approached even closer, the image faded, leaving the ruins, a mere shadow of the splendour that once stood there. Still unable to believe his eyes, he heard a sound behind him and turned. A few yards behind him stood an elderly woman, silently staring at him until she, too, vanished.

Given Alma's affinity for old buildings and "delving among the ruins," it is no wonder she couldn't leave her residence when it burned down. Perhaps she chooses to stay there and offer a glimpse of it to strangers who might appreciate what she so loved.

I had been to the Hermitage before that moonless night I partook in the Ghost Walk — but in full light of day. Even in the heat of the afternoon sun, I could feel something special, something powerful about the place. Standing in the presence of what remains of a large and spectacular building can do that to a person.

But in the thick of night, listening to Ghost Guide George stand in what was once the summer kitchen of the home, recounting eerie tales, much colder shivers ran down my spine. Forget about the ghosts themselves. Just thinking about how the site has, over the years, attracted cultists, Satanists, and other practitioners of the dark arts — drawn by its sheer power, by the legend of ghosts that haunt it, to perform black magic sacrifices and rituals under the light of a full moon — gave me the creeps.

As the tour continued on a trail around the Hermitage and back down the path to where we began, the high, quavering cry of a coyote echoed through the night, punctuating the primitive fear already well in play.

Of course, part of my mind still wonders if it really was a coyote. After all, it might just as well have been the mournful wail of William Black, forever lamenting his unrequited love, or of Alma, who will never again see her regent mansion and estate in its former glory.

CHAPTER SEVEN

AUCHMAR HOUSE

There is an old, lonely Gothic mansion at the busy corner of Fennel Avenue and West 5th in Hamilton. Though the traffic is heavy through this neighbourhood, not much happens at Auchmar House. And though huge cranes jut out into the sky from the massive construction site across the street, part of the new $1.5 billion in upgrades to St. Joe's psychiatric hospital, this mansion that was once a man's dream is left behind like some distant shadow of a memory.

Hidden behind an overgrowth of trees, Auchmar sits vacant, worn by time and neglect, mocked by the huge economic development taking place while it decays

Of the thousands of people who pass the building daily, many might shake their heads at its state, not knowing the full and rich history of it and its occupants; but others who pass, those who might have learned a bit more about the house, long-shrouded in mystery, perhaps shudder at the thought of what spirits might be looking back at them out of the dark and dirty windows, crying out in voices unheard over the heavy sounds of traffic and construction.

And wonder what stories those spirits might share if only given the chance.

Built between 1852 and 1854 on land that Isaac Buchanan (1810–1883) purchased, Auchmar was constructed in the Carpenter Gothic style of architecture, which is defined on Wikipedia as "a North American style-designation for an application of Gothic Revival architectural detailing and picturesque massing applied to wooden structures built by house-carpenters." Carpenter Gothic is a style that improvises upon features that were carved in stone in authentic Gothic architecture but with an emphasis on charm and quaintness.[1]

The name Auchmar was taken from the estate on Loch Lomond, Scotland, owned by Isaac Buchanan's family.[2] Born in Glasgow in 1810, Buchanan became an apprentice to a firm of Glasgow merchants in 1825 and a junior partner in a Montreal wholesale business they opened. He moved to York (Toronto) to be closer to his Upper Canada clients and in 1834 bought the business with his brother Peter.[3]

Buchanan served in the local militia during the Upper Canada Rebellion, was elected to the Legislative Assembly for the city of Toronto, helped establish the Free Church of Scotland in Canada West, and helped set up the Board of Trade. He sat as a member of the Parliament of United Canada for Toronto between 1841 and 1843 and for Hamilton between 1857 and 1865. He was also a director in the Great Western Railway in 1857 and became a writer of some note on the subjects of currency and trade, supporting protectionist policies. Buchanan is generally credited as being a formative influence on John A. Macdonald's national policy.[4, 5]

Buchanan's political interests distracted him from his business interests and, although he resigned his seat in 1865, his business failed in 1867. He sold his beloved Auchmar estate in Hamilton and received a government appointment in 1879, which sustained him through his later years. Buchanan died in Hamilton in 1883.[6]

During the years Buchanan lived in Auchmar, the resplendent house was visited by such notable historic figures as Sir John A. Macdonald (Canada's first prime minister), Sir

Allan MacNab (of Dundurn Castle), Pope John Paul II (when he was Cardinal), Lord and Lady Dufferin, and the Prince of Wales, who later became King Henry VII.[7]

Buchanan was an advocate that the town of Hamilton should be built on top of and not under the hill. Though his original intention was to build a summer residence, it is said that Buchanan, first witnessing the spectacular view upon climbing the escarpment, was so enamoured with the mountain location that he resolved to make it a permanent residence.[8] The vast acres surrounding the mansion were named Clairemont (from the French "clear mountain"),[9] which is a name that is still used today for a neighbourhood, a park, and a mountain road access.

The interior was finished in a beautifully grained softwood, and many of the inside walls were made with brick, ensuring a nearly fireproof home. Ten fireplaces were on the ground floor and a long hall in the shape of a Roman cross occupied the main floor. Stairways with bright, large windows ascended from each end, allowing for the free circulation of air.[10]

In a 1936 interview in the *Hamilton Spectator*, Elsie Buchanan (Isaac's daughter) said that originally there were glass-enclosed verandas running the length of the home's front and back and that her father was determined to experience the health benefits of the sunshine even when it was too cold to step outside. Years after, this same practice was used to combat tuberculosis, prompting Miss Buchanan to point out that her father was a thinker well ahead of his time. She also described the home as having a bathroom and a furnace from the very early days, both features that were not found in many residences during the 1850s. "Another proof that my father was ahead of his time," she said.[11]

The builders originally planned the ground floor with four large rooms of identical dimensions (18 x 20 feet). Then it was decided that the dining room be more generous in size, "in order to accommodate the lavish parties that the Buchanans intended to hold for government officials and political associates."[12]

When Buchanan died at the age of 73, Auchmar was sold to a military man from India by the name of Captain Trigg.[13] Trigg made a notable change while living there by converting the grand ballroom into a preaching hall, which was used for the congregation that gathered there every Sunday.[14]

Mrs. Alma Dick-Lauder, the last owner of the Hermitage before fire destroyed it (a featured subject in a previous chapter of this book), also wrote about this residence in the 1897 book *Wentworth Landmarks*, published by the Hamilton Spectator Press:

> The old family home of the Buchanan's is one of these set in the midst of a grand old grove of trees and looking quaint and beautiful as one approaches it. . . . From a distance it gives the impression of a walled-fort. . . . The whole place was vacant for several years after the Buchanan family moved into the city, and then a cultured English gentleman named Capt. Trigg became its owner. He has had repairs made, and while he remains there it is sure that the olden time beauty of the place will remain…. The hall is cathedral-like because its ceiling is Gothic. Nor is it gloomy, as one might imagine. The effect is not gloom; it is something different—a dim, religious light.[15]

James Buchanan, Isaac's fourth son, bought the property back in 1900. In 1926 the Buchanan family sold Auchmar to A.V. Young, who lived there with his family until September 1943.[16]

At that point it was rented to the Royal Canadian Air Force as a rehabilitation centre; the Second World War was raging in Europe and thus many hospitals were needed for the returning heroes. Auchmar's many rooms and long halls perfectly suited a hospital's needs.[17]

The ghosts of Auchmar are shrouded in a long-standing and complex series of mysteries.

The Hungarian Sisters of Social Service bought the mansion and land in 1945 for $32,000, converting the building and grounds into a religious retreat called the Holy Spirit Centre. They occupied Auchmar longer than any other resident, until 1999, when Auchmar was acquired by the City of Hamilton.[18]

One hundred and thirty-five years after Auchmar was built, the cast and crew of YTV's *Strange Days at Blake Holsey High* (also known as Black Hole High) converged on the grounds to begin filming.[19]

One can only speculate that, with such a long legacy of so many different residents — including returning war veterans and those in need of religious respite — many different spirits might haunt the halls. But nowhere in the long history of the building are any ghostly visitations or sightings revealed. Could it be the nature of those who occupied the building and their unwillingness to reveal secrets housed within the walls, or were the spirits suddenly awakened, disturbed by the transition of the once-magnificent estate to occupation by such a different type of crew?

And this is where the speculative tales of this building and its ghosts begin.

Two workmen from the YTV television crew were carrying heavy equipment from the basement to the main floor. Holding a large box, the two men looked up just before reaching the first floor landing to see a young girl waiting at the top. They looked away only for a moment, glancing at one another as if to confirm they had both seen her. When they both looked back only a second later, the little girl had vanished.[20]

This strange little girl seems to be one of the most active ghosts within the house. Crew members have heard her voice from the second floor while working on the main floor.

At times she is said to be heard happily giggling, as if she is playing and laughing in the carefree manner of a child. Other times her soft cries or blood-curdling screams are heard echoing through the empty nighttime hallways.

A local Hamilton woman recalls "having a personal meeting" with the little girl when she was a child and visiting Auchmar with her father (a city official at the time). Shortly after the nuns moved out, she and her father were given a personal tour of the mansion. Bored with the history being shared on the tour, the young lady slipped away from the adults and started exploring.

Up on the second floor by herself, she heard the soft giggle of another little girl. Intrigued, she looked around to determine where the other child was, but could see nobody. The sound of giggling continued, confusing her, because it sounded as if it were getting closer. Still, she stood alone in the hallway. Finally, a subtle gust of cold moved over her, and a voice in her ear spoke the words "play with me" to her. She immediately ran down the stairs and into her father's arms.[21]

The spirit of a woman has also been seen in the basement, floating throughout the vaulted stone rooms. Many crew members and actors from the YTV television show have also commented on strange feelings while in the basement.

Daniel Cumerlato of Haunted Hamilton has mentioned that the most noticeable energy comes from the basement area. During a personal tour with the folks of Doors Open Hamilton several years ago, both he and Stephanie felt it. "It was almost like you expected to see an uninvited guest waiting just around the corner while moving through the small confined rooms of Auchmar's basement," he said.[22]

Over the years, various objects from the mansion have mysteriously disappeared, dogs brought onto the set of *Strange Days at Blake Holsey High* have refused to enter certain corridors, and hanging lights would start to swing on their own in the absence of any breeze. In a 2002 interview with the *Hamilton Spectator*'s Jeff Mahoney, Lawrence Bayne, one of the actors from the television show, spoke about his eerie experiences at Auchmar one night when, instead of heading to his home in Toronto, he slept in his dressing room. "Well, you tell me," Bayne asked in that interview, "how does a door that is locked and bolted suddenly swing open in the middle of the night?"[23]

Mitch Ness, director for *Strange Days at Blake Holsey High*, reported several of his strange experiences on the set of the show at Auchmar to Daniel. One recurring encounter took place near the stairs, where there seemed to be a malicious spirit offering ghostly shoves as if to either harm or frighten off intruders. In one such occurrence, the script supervisor was shoved by those invisible hands while standing at the monitors and watching a rehearsal.

Two grips had a similar experience while heading up a set of stairs that curved up to the left to a small room. Rohan, the best boy grip, and Ross, the key grip, were heading up the stairs, when Rohan was pushed so strongly that he fell back hard against Ross and the two of them almost tumbled down the stairs. They found the room at the top of the stairs closed and locked tight; Rohan was unable to figure out the source of the unseen hands he felt pushing him.

Two of the YTV television show's effects team encountered a strange apparition in the basement. Separately, but within minutes of one another, both Sean and Gary were in the basement for an episode involving a furnace (which they had constructed in the basement), when they spied the female spectre who is said to be in the basement. In the main hallway of the basement, a white figure, what looked to them like a nun, moved from one room to another, footless and floating along the floor.

Security guards who worked on the set of the television show were kept busy tracking down phantoms on many a night, from the echo of footsteps in the upstairs corridor to doors slamming. Commonly, a door leading to a small balcony would be found wide open, even after one of the guards had closed and locked it.[24]

In 2005 the television series *Ghost Trackers* filmed the thirteenth and final episode of their first season at Auchmar, in which one of the competitors felt an invisible finger brush past.[25]

Still owned by the City of Hamilton, and a popular stop on the annual Doors Open Hamilton tours of landmark buildings, Auchmar remains a historical building of cultural interest under threat. For years the debate about preserving the important historical estate and the economic challenges of doing so has raged on.

For its part, the mansion continues to erode under the weight of time and the elements while the restless spirits inside flit about, holding vigilant to their shadowy posts, reminders of the flurry of activity, the richness of life, hope, and history that once coursed through these now-empty rooms.

CHAPTER EIGHT

WOODEND

John Heslop's bloodstain on the floor at the base of the stairs of Woodend would still be visible if not for a strategically placed rug.[1] Murdered in 1891,[2] his spirit allegedly still roams the building, forever bemoaning the fact that his killers were not brought to justice.

The son of Robert and Diana Heslop, John Heslop was born in Cumberland, England, in 1812. Just a few years later, his family moved to North America, with the family living in New Brunswick, Washington, and Virginia before settling in Ancaster and purchasing land there in 1842.[3]

In his book *Murder: Twelve True Stories of Homicide in Canada*, Edward Butts describes a time when Heslop supported William Lyon Mackenzie, carrying messages back and forth for the rebels and personally escorting Mackenzie through the Ancaster area. Butts explains that Heslop managed to avoid arrest for treason, settle back into the life of a farmer, and do well for himself.[4]

Heslop was married to Elizabeth Aikman in 1844 and had a daughter named Sarah Ann, who was born the following year. In 1851 he became the first warden of Wentworth County and the first reeve of Ancaster Township.[5] In the early 1870s, he was appointed clerk and treasurer of the township.[6]

Originally constructed in 1862, the stately beauty of Woodend's Victorian Gothic revival style — with the use of a large three-gabled front facade adding depth to the building, its steep roof, and delicate barge — all reflected Heslop's taste and sense of grandeur.[7] Set on the top of a hill near Mineral Springs Road, the stone building was surrounded by large, beautiful gardens. It would instantly be seen as a tranquil and bountiful home, which is perhaps one of the things that led thieves to it one fateful night.

Shortly after 1:00 a.m. on January 27, 1891, John, his wife Elizabeth, and their daughter Sarah were all fast asleep, when they were suddenly awoken by a crash from downstairs.[8] Leaping out of his bed, Heslop met two masked men who had broken into the house through the back door using a piece of cordwood as a battering ram. The men had assumed that, because Heslop was the town treasurer, sums of money were kept in the house.[9]

Rather agile for a man of his age, Heslop wielded a chair against the intruders, but was shot and killed instantly, his body tumbling down to the base of the stairs.[10]

Several men were arrested, and Jack Bartram and Jack Lottridge were put on trial for the murder, but due to a combination of conflicting evidence, inconsistent alibis, and the inability of Elizabeth and Sarah to properly identify the masked men, the jury found them not guilty.[11]

The murder, its trial, and the "not guilty" verdict remained a sensation in Ancaster for many years.[12] Heslop's wife died the following year at the age of seventy-two, and Sarah lived in the house until she sold it in 1909.[13]

The building is now home to the Hamilton Region Conservation Authority, the Hamilton region's largest environmental management agency, which owns or manages about 4,000 hectares (10,000 acres) of environmentally significant land, as well as recreational land, and promotes environmental stewardship and education.[14]

Courtesy of Stephanie Lechniak

Woodend, a historic mansion on Mineral Springs Road in Ancaster, is said to be very much alive with an unhappy ghost of the past.

It is fascinating that an entity that promotes and protects is now the occupant of a home in which the owner, in his attempt to protect his family, was murdered in cold blood. Perhaps the murder's classification as an unsolved crime is why legends of John Heslop's ghost abound.

It has been said that the ghost of Heslop and of his daughter, who witnessed his murder, can be seen as an orb in photographs of the stairway. People have also reported strange dragging noises coming from the attic as well as footsteps moving through the house.

A cleaner has reported her vacuum cleaner being mysteriously unplugged and then plugged back in and pictures constantly being tilted at strange angles.[15]

Could these reports be evidence that John Heslop's ghost remains in the home, forever destined to restlessly move about the building, unable to attain the peace of a final rest in knowing that his murderers will never be brought to justice?

CHAPTER NINE

BURKHOLDER CEMETERY

Jacob Burkholder was born in Ementhan, Bern, Switzerland, in 1747, and he married Sophia de Roche in September 1765 in Pennsylvania, U.S.A.[1]

In October 1794 Jacob and his wife were one of the first pioneering families to settle in the Hamilton Mountain area,[2] establishing the Burkholder settlement on the Mohawk Trail. They also established a cemetery on a portion of land, and, sadly, one of the first interments to the Burkholder Cemetery was that of their son Joseph Burkholder, who died after falling off of a roof.[3]

In the early 1800s, people from surrounding neighbourhoods were bringing deceased family members to the cemetery to be placed beside Burkholder family members; due to the Burkholder's religious beliefs and them being so community-minded, nobody was refused.[4]

The epitaph on the stone marking the resting place of Christian Burkholder, who died in 1843, reads:

REMEMBER FRIEND, AS YOU PASS BY

AS YOU ARE NON SO ONCE WAS I

AS I AM NOW, SO YOU WILL BE

PREPARE FOR DEATH AND FOLLOW ME[5]

It is very much a *memento mori*–style message. Integral to some forms of art and literature, *memento mori* is a Latin phrase that translates to "remember your mortality" or "remember you will die."

The epitaph and the sentiment fit well with the legends regarding the Burkholder Cemetery, which speak of an unearthly orb of light commonly seen floating there, as if to announce that another soul has been claimed.

In an article written for the Haunted Hamilton website about Burkholder Cemetery, Chris Mills wrote about an experience he had there.

> Without any prior knowledge of this historical cemetery's past, I paid my first ever visit inside its gates. It was mid-afternoon, and the sun was shining brightly as I arrived on location. To be completely honest, I'd never experienced such an eerie feeling entering a cemetery before. The moment I stepped inside the main gate, the sky became overcast and a strong wind had developed. My legs began to shake nervously as I walked past the graves.[6]

The bizarre and strange feeling that overcame Mills isn't surprising, particularly given the long history of strange reports from the site.

Spectral lights over graves or where murderous activities took place are not uncommon. In relation to Burkholder Cemetery, however, their presence has historically been associated with the premonition of death.

It is said that a light would shine in the dead of night while the townsfolk slept. It signified a departed soul and was alleged to light up over the adjacent Burkholder Church and hover along the length of the roof before floating quietly into the graveyard. Similar eerie lights were said to occasionally have been seen hovering above the house of the departed and take similar paths to the grave, as illustrating the path between life and death taking place.[7]

The typical path of soul departing from body and body being laid to rest in a grave has sometimes been shaken and turned around.

Grave robbing was a not-uncommon practice, particularly in a town with medical practitioners. Corpses for medical study could be extremely hard to come by back in those days. A doctor could either eagerly wait in the hopes that convicted criminals would be put to death and their bodies donated to the pursuit of medicine, or they could find another way....

In the dead of night, a local doctor dug up freshly interred bodies to use for medical study. He would have gotten away with his crimes if not for a female servant who shared stories with the locals about the strange pieces of flesh she found in the wash-boiler of the doctor's home.[8]

Over the years, many photographs and videos have been taken at the cemetery, each photographer anxious to try to document evidence of the legendary lights.

But the main thing that all who visit this historic site are witness to are the quiet graves, some anonymous stones, and others with eerily prophetic messages for the living — all reminders that one day those looking upon the stones will, too, inevitably pass into death.

CHAPTER TEN

WHITEHERN MANSION

"Ghosts walk the grounds of this garden — island of tranquil beauty, oasis within bustling urban core," Eleanore Kosydar writes in her 2005 poem, "Gardens of Whitehern." Kosydar was referring to Mary McQuesten's role when, later in the poem, she writes, "Mother Mary's hand is everywhere."[1] McQuesten created what is recognized as one of the finest heritage gardens in Canada, and the profound effect the beautiful historic garden still has despite the encroachment of urban development on the surrounding land.

Of course, the McQuesten family legacy left behind much more than a beautiful and stately garden. The family was instrumental in establishing the Royal Botanical Gardens, McMaster University's move from Toronto to Hamilton, and the Queen Elizabeth Way highway.[2]

Whitehern (originally named Willow Bank) was the McQuesten family home for 116 years, from 1852 until the death of the final remaining family member, Reverend Calvin McQuesten.[3]

The City of Hamilton describes Whitehern as being "prominently situated in a walled garden" on the corner of

Jackson Street West and MacNab Street South in Hamilton. Whitehern, built in 1850, is a Late Classical house that remains an outstanding example of a mid-nineteenth-century urban estate.[4]

Today, the house has "a multi-layered character that reflects the alterations made by three generations of the McQuesten family. It contains elements from many time periods — Georgian, Victorian, and Edwardian — all overlaid with original possessions dating up to 1939 when the Honourable Thomas McQuesten was minister of highways."[5]

In 1839 Dr. Calvin McQuesten gave up a successful career in medicine in the United States in favour of moving to Canada, aligning his fortunes with Hamilton.[6] McQuesten established an iron foundry and, as a skilled businessman, was able to amass a sizeable family fortune over a twenty-year period. Most of that fortune was lost by Calvin's son, Isaac, who invested in manufacturing ventures that failed. Involved in a very destructive pattern of alcoholism and despair, Isaac died suddenly at the age of forty on March 7, 1888, reportedly as the result of a combination of a sleeping draught and alcohol. It was publicly rumoured that he committed suicide.[7]

However, Isaac's own son, Thomas, who was six years old at the time of his father's death, was destined to make significantly positive and enduring marks on the Hamilton region during his life.

Mary Baker McQuesten raised her family alone in Whitehern (which is a Scottish term meaning "White House"). Thomas absorbed his mother's desire to contribute to the fabric of society, received his law degree in 1907, and devoted his life to politics and public projects that would better the human condition.[8]

McQuesten died in 1948 from intestinal cancer, and in 1968, following the death of the last surviving family member, Whitehern was officially handed over to the City of Hamilton and is today preserved as a museum.[9]

The beautiful Whitehern Historic House and Garden is a feature stop on Haunted Hamilton's popular Downtown Hamilton Ghost Walk.

Rumours of haunting at Whitehern persist, mostly due to stories from people who spend a great deal of time there. A worker at Whitehern has claimed to have experienced many strange and unexplainable things in her time there, such as the voice of a woman lightly singing from the second floor, accompanied by the sounds of a piano.[10]

On one occasion, this worker was locking up for the night and thought she heard a radio playing from the second floor. She went up the stairs to turn it off, but it stopped before she could get to it. It was only then she realized there wasn't a radio on the second floor at all.[11] This ethereal singing and music is usually credited to a wife of Thomas's brother, who was a soprano. But the legacy of mental illness afflicting the family, something Mary Baker often worried about, might be what has led to some other strange encounters in Whitehern.

Another staff member who used to work in the museum relayed a story to the folks at Haunted Hamilton. One day, while all alone in the museum, the employee was walking down the main staircase toward the main floor when she was violently shoved aside. She was pushed so hard that she had to brace herself against the wall to keep from falling down the stairs. As she regained her footing, she saw the shadowy figure of a man, grey in colour, rushing past her, down the stairs, and out the front door.[12]

In her book, *The Life Writings of Mary Baker McQuesten: Victorian Matriarch*, Mary Anderson, a noted Whitehern and McQuesten scholar, notes the apparent Victorian Gothic elements in the McQuesten family's tale: "We can add a wicked stepmother, a madwoman in the attic, a tragic heroine, inherited mental disorders, institutionalization, social stigma and secrecy."[13]

Those walking through the beautiful gardens are said to feel an intensely powerful emotion — and not just that from the sheer beauty and majesty originally instilled under Mary Baker's hand. There is a lingering sense of the powerful and important family that once called Whitehern their home, of their various hopes, highlights, and hardships through multiple generations.

This historically significant and picturesque home, which sits at 41 James Street, is certainly no stranger to incredible struggles and intense emotions, all of which can lead to echoes of the past randomly exerting their presence on the here and now.

Chapter Eleven

MOUNT ALBION FALLS

Alma Dick-Lauder opens chapter 15 of her book, *Pen and Pencil Sketches of Wentworth Landmarks*, with the following: "There's a fascination frantic in a ruin that's romantic." She goes on to describe an area that is most impressive when the nights are moonlit, and she writes of a half-hidden pass filled with strange, lurking figures and a suppressed murmur of voices:

> We know the figures are only shadows cast by the sombre swaying pines, and the voices are the voices of nature embodied in the trees, and running water; yet heard in connection with the idea of a fortress, they make us think of soldiers preparing for the attack, in obedience of orders passed along the line. Aided by imagination the sounds take meaning and grow distinctly on the ear. A ray of moonlight flashes on some bright object among the shadows. Firearms surely! And instinctively we turn, half expecting to hear an awful salute from the fortress. An owl hoots dismally that weird note which turns the thoughts

to death and disaster. The grey bird flits past the face of a rock that rises to a height of 80 feet, and from the top of which a young girl cast herself to death, rather than face desertion on the part of her lover, who, when the wedding feast was ready, failed to appear. Out of the gloom where the bird has vanished comes another mournful cry and the gorge is filled with ghostly echoes.[1]

Alma was, of course, writing about Albion Falls, a classical cascading waterfall of just under 20 metres (62 feet) in the Red Hill Valley in Hamilton.[2] The cascading steps of the waterfall begin on Mud Street and the lower end is found at the south end of King's Forest Park. The falls and the area are stunning in their picturesque glory. But beneath the postcard-perfect glimpses of natural beauty lie shadows that crawl out from the pages of history and up the spines of those who stand nearby and reflect on the tragedy and horrors that occurred there.

The drop of the ravine has been dubbed "Lover's Leap" due to the legend of a young Jane Riley, who, disappointed by the unreturned love from Joseph Rousseau, flung herself from the steep cliff at the top of Albion Falls.[3] Her love and the extreme disappointment she faced was known throughout the village of Mount Albion, which was an important community, as it featured a gristmill, blacksmith shops, taverns, a church, and a general store.[4]

The village owed its existence to William Alexander Davis (1741–1843), a United Empire Loyalist who left North Carolina to fight alongside the British in the American Revolution. Davis was granted 2,300 acres in Barton and Saltfleet Townships, including five hundred acres around Albion Falls. The Davis estate consisted of a tannery, an orchard, a general store, a distillery, taverns, a church, a sawmill, and a gristmill. The two names lent the area the name Albion Mills (Albion being the poetic name for Britain). In 1880 the village was renamed Mount Albion.[5]

Courtesy of Stephanie Lechniak

Legends of the Lover's Leap aren't the only things that haunt the picturesque ravine at Albion Falls.

The *Hamilton Spectator* archives note an incident that took place in 1897 near a house not far from the falls. A gentleman and two ladies were driving in a horse-drawn carriage, when the horses suddenly snorted in fear and stopped in their tracks. There, alongside the carriage, they saw a ghostly figure appear. Out of either fear or in an attempt to protect the ladies he was travelling with, the man lashed his horsewhip into the air toward the figure, but the whip passed right through and the ghostly image faded. They then proceeded on their journey and they saw nothing more, but it frightened them enough to share their eerie tale.

About half a mile down the valley from Albion Falls, two streams join together. One is from Buttermilk Falls and the other from the Albion Falls, or the Mill Falls as it was called at the time. Below this merger of the two streams there was a dam and a primitive sawmill. When a quarrel broke out among some of the workers, one of the men was killed. Local legend holds that for the fifty years following his death, his home was haunted. People continued to report seeing his ghost wandering about the house, hovering over the stream near where he died, travelling along the road, or flitting about the woods.

Years later, in the height of these legends, a woodcutter who lived in that very house spent the day drinking at Mount Albion's Black Horse Tavern. While he was out, his mischievous neighbours slaughtered a pig, dressed it up in some clothes, and then hung it in a tree adjacent to his home. At midnight, when the inebriated man returned to the dwelling, he saw the hanging pig. His mind immediately flashed to the stories of the ghost reported to have haunted the building and the area, but rather than take flight, the alcohol in his system gave him a bout of courage, and he stormed up to the "ghost" and struck it with all of his might. He ended up breaking his right arm and putting an end to both the ghost stories and that particular type of prank, at least on that spot and in that era.

In 1907, the owner of the old mill, Robert Grassie, fell to his death in the wheel pit near the falls. The mill, which was eventually torn down in 1915, was never run again after he died.[6]

The aforementioned tragedy of Jane Riley took place in the early 1900s. Jane and Joseph Rousseau were said to have been childhood friends who fell in love with one another. It was Joseph's mother, however, who did not like the young girl and was against their courtship and plans for marriage.

Heartbroken and devastated that she could not have the man she so loved, on a fateful moonlit night in September 1915, Jane threw herself into the dark depths of the ravine. It is rumoured that on some nights, perhaps similar moonlit nights to the one in which she took her life, you can hear her soft cries echoing from the gorge below.

A poet known only as Slater commemorated the events of that tragedy in verse:

Alas, poor Jane Riley
For Joseph she did die
By jumping off that dizzying brink
Full sixty cubits high[7]

It was reported that Joseph's mother said of the event, "Let the blame rest on my shoulders." Some years later, the still-healthy woman suddenly shrieked, "Jane's hand is on my shoulder!" and collapsed to the floor, dead.[8]

Another interesting aspect of the area involved organized crime. One of the most significant mobsters in Canadian history, Canada's version of Al Capone, Rocco Perri (1887–1944) was known as "Canada's King of the Bootleggers." And mobster activity typically comes with some sort of body count.[9] It's reported that people who got in Perri's way received a one-way ticket to the King's Forest or the mountain brow. The dense bushes, jutting rocks of the escarpment, and twisted trails were supposedly an excellent place to dispose of corpses.

The bodies of Joseph Boytowicz and Fred Genesee were found in the area in 1924, allegedly victims of Perri and his gang. On November 6 of that year, a group of boy scouts found a decomposed body concealed in some bushes on the escarpment nearby. It was the body of Boytowicz, who had been missing for over three months. The thirty-eight-year-old's skull had been fractured. Eight days later, Genesee's body was found on the Stoney Creek mountainside. His body had been pushed over the edge of a small cliff and lay caught in bushes about fifteen feet down the slope. Blunt force trauma was evident on the right side of his head, and the blow had shattered his right eye socket and dislodged the eyeball. Cause of death was ruled to be strangulation.[10]

The police, aware of an ongoing bootleg war and rumoured death threats, felt there was a connection between the two murders. A small media circus ensued, with local reporters speculating wildly about the involvement of both men and the manner by which they suggested they had crossed paths with Perri and his bootleg gang.

Perri was found to not be responsible for either death.

On April 23, 1943, Rocco headed out for a walk "to shake a headache" and never came home. Although Hamilton police alluded to having information that he could be found in cement at the bottom of Hamilton Bay, they suggested he would likely not ever be found until the bay was drained. For all anybody knows, the body might very well be buried somewhere on the side of Hamilton Mountain.

Twenty years after the gruesome discovery of two bodies in that area, an even more horrifying "body dump" took place, one that would send the media into an even more dramatic frenzy and send shockwaves through the entire Hamilton community. It is an event that has been turned into countless books, a stage play, and several different films.

Known as the *Torso Murder*, the case of Evelyn Dick remains one of the most sensationalized events in Canadian crime history. A well-known schoolyard song from the time (which inspired the Forgotten Rebels in their 1989 song "Evelyn Dick") went like this:

> You cut off his legs ...
> You cut off his arms ...
> You cut off his head ...
> How could you Mrs. Dick?
> How could you Mrs. Dick?[11]

A song entitled "Over the Hill" was written by Marcy Italiano and her husband Giasone, a pair raised in Hamilton not far from where the Dick murder took place. It appears on *Gruesome*, which is a soundtrack CD to promote the book *Johnny Gruesome* by Gregory Lamberson. The CD features songs based on the

novel as well as other eerie things like ghosts and monsters —
people like Evelyn Dick falling into the "monster" category. It
takes the element of morbid humour a bit further in its opening:

> He did not know
> When he came home
> That you'd be there
> With a cleaver in the air
> You chopped up John
> Oh, did you have fun?
> You said you didn't kill
> Threw him over the hill[12]

Born on October 13, 1920, in Beamsville, Ontario, Evelyn
Dick later moved with her parents to Hamilton. There is
evidence that her father was abusive, struggled with alcohol
abuse, and might also have been siphoning funds from the
Hamilton Street Railway, where he worked. Evelyn tried hard to
fit in with the higher-class in town and was consistently at the
heart of rumours. She was often seen in the company of older
men and continually being caught in outright lies, such as her
claims to be married to a man stationed overseas, who was never
proven to exist.[13]

Evelyn married John Dick in 1945 after a very quick
courtship and apparently engaged in her first extramarital affair
within the first week of marriage.

On Saturday March 16, 1946, a group of five children
found what they thought was a human body partway down the
escarpment in the Albion Falls area. They scrambled up the hill
and blocked the roadway on the top with a human chain, hoping
to stop the first car that arrived and alert them of their find. The
first adults on the scene insisted that what they likely saw was the
body of a slaughtered pig, but the children insisted it was human
and was wearing a shirt.

What they had found was the torso of an adult male. The head, arms, and legs were missing and to this day have not been found. A deep abdominal wound suggested that somebody had tried to cut the torso itself in two.

A report in the *Hamilton Spectator* read, "Clothed only in an undershirt and shorts, the torso of an unidentified man with the head, legs and arms missing, was found ... one half-mile from Albion Falls, about 10 o'clock this morning ... The gruesome find was made by a group of children ... out for a Saturday morning hike."[14] The body was confirmed to be that of John Dick, who had been reported missing by his cousin on March 6.

Evelyn Dick was immediately questioned but denied knowing anything or having anything to do with her husband's murder. Investigation revealed that a Packard Evelyn had borrowed from a Bill Landeg was returned to him with blood covering the seat and bloody clothing in the back. Her excuse involved a companion who had cut herself and made the mess, but the blood was found to be the same type as John Dick's.[15]

When the blood was revealed likely to be that of her husband, Evelyn told police that an unknown man had called her and told her of John having gotten a woman pregnant, further adding he had received what was coming to him for his actions. She explained the man asked to meet and gave her a large sack containing "part of John." She claimed to have driven this man and his sack to the dumping site.[16]

The sultry-eyed, black-haired, beautiful woman found herself at the centre of one of the most publicized trials in Canadian crime history. Hundreds of Hamiltonians appeared to witness the trial, packing lunches and shoving their way to get a good spot, and those involved in the case became unwilling celebrities of their time.

Evelyn reportedly yawned and drew sketches while in the courtroom, smiled openly for photographers, and uttered phrases such as "My public is waiting to see me." Taxi drivers fawned over the beautiful woman, eagerly competing to escort her to court, and her admirers sent her flowers and cards.[17, 18, 19]

She later changed her story and suggested the involvement of killers hired by Bill Bohozuk. Evelyn Dick was found guilty of John Dick's death through involvement in participating and planning the murder and was sentenced to hang on January 7, 1947 — but the case was overturned on appeal due to the fact that Evelyn's statements were improperly admitted into evidence.

Though acquitted of the murder of her husband, the police later got her on a second charge of manslaughter related to her newborn son, who was found encased in cement in a suitcase in her family home. She was sentenced to life in prison but was paroled after a dozen years.

Evelyn Dick has not been seen since her parole, but some suggest that her husband's tortured ghost still prowls the mountainside near Albion Falls in a futile attempt to collect his still-missing body parts. John Dick is just one of many lost souls wandering the area, reminders of the accidents, murders, and suicides it has been played to.

CHAPTER TWELVE

DUNDAS DISTRICT ELEMENTARY SCHOOL

Actor Dave Thomas graduated Dundas District Elementary School in 1967. He and his brother, Ian, who graduated a few years later and went on in his musical career to win a Juno, are perhaps the best-known graduates from this school.

Some years after leaving Dundas District, Dave Thomas worked on *Second City Television* (*SCTV*) with a colleague named Joe Flaherty. Flaherty played a character known as Count Floyd, a low-budget local-television "horror" show host. Though Thomas lives in California, his long-time colleague Flaherty still lives in the Hamilton area. Given the legends surrounding Dundas District Elementary School, one wonders if Flaherty might occasionally be tempted to don his old costume, stand on the grounds of the school his comedic pal used to attend, and in his "Transylvanian" accent, say something like, "Gather 'round, kids, and be prepared to hear a scary story about the ghosts and pranks that took place here." He would, of course, finish with his trademark eerie werewolf howl (despite being dressed as a vampire).

The reason the fictitious host of the equally fictitious *Monster Chiller Horror Theatre* might be appropriate to introduce this haunted school isn't just due to the tie-in with a locally born alumni. The tales of this particular site range from the truly tragic and horrific to a series of pranks that don't seem to have stopped upon death of the alleged prankster.

The Dundas District Public School stands vacant on the former Highway 8 at the foot of the Niagara Escarpment. This landmark building was the perfect scenic and easily accessible location for students in both Dundas and Flamborough.[1]

Originally built as the Dundas District High School and designed by Hamilton architect William J. Walsh, the goal was to mimic a Collegiate Gothic style. Budget limitations resulted in the completed building not looking as grand as originally intended in the design; however, the result was a well-proportioned three-storey building of rug brick with finely carved stone detailing.[2]

The Gothic stone ornamentation on the building includes decorative crests, door lintels marking separate entrances for girls and boys, as well as pinnacles and gargoyles. Legend has it that gargoyles are meant to scare off, or protect the building from, any evil or harmful spirits — but in this particular case, though much of the original architecture maintains a high degree of architectural integrity, a testament to the original designers and builders, and the gargoyles still stand watch over the building, it seems as if their mission has failed.[3]

Stylistically, this abandoned school might be compared to other Hamilton schools built in the same era, such as Westdale High and George R. Allen.[4] The building dates back to 1849 when the Dundas Select Academy, a private grammar school on Ogilvie Street, was established. The original building at 397 King Street West was constructed in 1928 on the former mill property donated by Robert and Frank Fisher. The brothers agreed to donate the property containing the Fisher Paper Mill (Gore Mills) as well as the vacant lot on the opposite side of King Street. They stipulated that the property must be kept in perpetuity for educational and public playground use.[5]

Courtesy of Stephanie Lechniak.

A historic train wreck and a bizarre pact formed by a group of custodians are tied to the strange occurrences at Dundas District Public School. Is the very ground it stands on still cursed?

The building operated as a high school until it was closed in 1982. Between 1987 and 1989, it became the temporary home for students of Dundas Central Public when their building was closed due to safety concerns. On November 5, 2007, Dundas District was closed, just a few months after it was deemed a historic site and was to be preserved.[6]

The boarded-up building at 397 King Street West currently sits unoccupied — at least by those among the living. As legend explains, there's likely more than one restless spirit that occupies the spot.

Going back to December of 1934, you'll see a shockingly tragic scene, one that a December 26 article in the *Hamilton Spectator* refers to as "the starkest tragedy that has ever darkened Hamilton's Christmas."

On a fateful Christmas Day in 1935, engineer Norman Devine pulled the CNR *Holiday Special* out of the Dundas Station and was heading eastbound toward Toronto for the holidays. On board were 365 passengers.

The train had been experiencing some minor mechanical problems, and with another train's approach on the schedule, the *Holiday Special* was stopped and diverted to a side track about 190 metres east of Dundas Station. However, a series of human errors and failures to observe signals led to the forward brakeman, Edward Lynch, to not be aware that the train had been moved to a side track.

Shortly after, due to engine issues, Lynch was walking back to the station to call for a new locomotive when he spotted a light in the distance — CNR No. 16, the *Maple Leaf Flyer*, on its scheduled run from Detroit to Montreal. Sent into a panic, and thinking the *Maple Leaf Flyer* was going to crash into the *Holiday Special*, Lynch rushed to the switch, unlocked it, and threw it open. Believing he had just prevented a horrific crash, he had inadvertently done just the opposite.

The speeding train crashed into the *Holiday Special*, smashing the rear car almost completely, destroying half of the second car, and shooting the third car up on its end. The fourth car was also damaged from the impact. Splinters and screams shot into the air, the terrifying soundtrack of mayhem audible to people in the village below.

The lights on the passenger cars went out as passengers were flung forward from the impact, some of them tossed out into the winter night. Chaos ensued in the darkness as fire broke out on the demolished rear car. Passengers were trapped in various locations of the wreck, and for several hours nearby rescue workers who arrived at the scene and medical personnel who happened to be on the train set about tending to the injured. Due to the almost complete darkness, the rescue efforts went to those whose groans and screams of pain could be detected among the wreckage.[7]

Either side of the tracks was littered with injured people and dead bodies. In an article published in the *Hamilton Spectator* on

December 31, 1993, Brian Henley wrote, "What followed was a hellish scene. Pandemonium broke out as surviving passengers crawled from the wreck, steam pipes burst scalding the trapped, and the right-of-way was littered with the bodies of the dead."

Stan Nowak, president of Dundas Valley Historical Society, similarly describes it in a November 12, 2004, article published in the *Ancaster News* as a "grisly scene of horrible death and suffering," with many passengers "trapped inside the twisted wreckage of the rear cars."

Edward Lynch was arrested and charged with manslaughter for his involvement in the accident. In January of 1935, after a great deal of confusing and conflicting testimony, the jury found Mr. Lynch not guilty.[8]

During that fateful night, Hamilton's old CNR passenger station on Stuart Street was used to hold and transfer patients to the hospital on Barton Street. An article in the *Hamilton Spectator* at the time described the site as resembling a clearing station behind the lines following an engagement in the First World War. Rumours continue to spread about the basement of the Dundas District School being used as a morgue to house the dead, despite assurances from groups such as the Dundas Historical Society that it is a myth.

Certainly, due to the chaos and confusion in the dark that night, some of the real facts might never be known, and it is entirely possible that, even for a limited time, the basement might have been used in this manner. But even if it was not, many experts in the field of supernatural investigation would agree that the proximity of the location might be enough for the intense experience of pain, suffering, and horror to leave an indelible psychic impression that continues to be felt at the location of the school.

Something, after all, has to explain why so many people have experienced strange and unexplainable events at that site. Something has to be behind the eerie noises, banging on lockers, and other poltergeist-like occurrences reported there.

An October 29, 2004, story in the *Ancaster News* by Erin Rankin entitled "Hair-Raising Local Legends Live On" spotlights strange things happening through an interview with Peter Greenberg, who was a principal at the school for five years.

Greenberg shared a story of when he came to work in the vacant school early one Saturday morning and the security guard warned him that someone might be inside, because the motion detector had gone off. The building was searched but nobody was found. Shortly after he had started working on some paperwork, he heard locker doors banging and clanging. Believing that vandals had indeed broken in, he called the police and immediately left the building.

When the police arrived, Greenberg went back into the building with one of the sergeants while the other officers waited outside. The thought was that the two men's entrance would frighten the kids out of the building and the awaiting officers outside would catch them.

As Greenberg and the sergeant approached the third floor, they could hear a crashing noise echoing through the halls; it sounded as if things were being thrown around and glass was being smashed. But when they got to the third floor and opened the door, the noise suddenly stopped, nothing was out of place or damaged, and there was no sign of any mischievous kids on the premises.[9]

One wonders if the banging and crashing Greenberg and others have heard might have been audible psychic echoes of the tragic events that occurred on that fateful December night in 1934.

Greenberg also spoke about custodians at the school who told stories of having left work undone only to return some time later and discover it had been completed. He also shared the fact that most of the custodians refused to go to the third floor after dark.[10]

He was referring, of course, to the legends of a former custodian by the name of Russell and a bizarre promise or pact that was made.

In 1954 there was a group of five men who worked quite closely as custodians at the school and shared convictions about being hard-working and dedicated to their tasks. Russell was the name of the man mostly responsible for maintaining the third floor of the building. He took great pride in keeping fastidious care of the school and his area in particular — offering the service, cleanliness, and attention to detail that one might expect in the parliament buildings, a mansion, or a palace.[11]

Russell, however, was as known for his perfectionism and attention to detail as he was for his fondness of jokes and playing pranks on his fellow workers, and he developed quite the reputation to that end. It was Russell who suggested that he and the other four make a simple pact: whoever died first would keep up the fun by coming back to haunt the school and prove to the others that there was indeed life after death.[12]

As it turns out, Russell was the first of the group to die and to, naturally, have played the role as set forth in the pact.

In an article in the *Hamilton Spectator* in October 2006, Suzanne Bourret interviewed two custodians at the Dundas District Public School, Veronika Lessard and Tony Vermeer, who shared their experiences. They mentioned having the ominous feeling of being watched as well as having heard voices and seen strange shadows moving while working in the supposedly vacant building.

Lessard, who worked at the school for more than six years, shared the story of how one evening she had left a bucket of water on the third floor before heading down to the first floor to have supper with the other custodians. When she returned, the entire floor had been washed and the bucket was still in the spot she had left it.

She also spoke about a time when, during the March break, she was up on a ladder, cleaning some lights, when she heard the clanking of keys. She had thought it was Tony setting out to tease her. (They both had been familiar with the legends of Russell.) She called out for whoever was there to show himself, and the shadowy form of a tall, lanky man jingling his keys passed by the door and offered her one of the biggest smiles she'd ever seen, before walking out of the room and vanishing. "I'll never forget that sight," Lessard said, believing that what she had seen was the ghost of Russell himself.

One evening both Lessard and Vermeer were leaving the otherwise vacant building when they heard the voice of a little old lady calling out from upstairs. From the top of the darkened stairway, they could hear an old lady calling out, "Help me!" They knew enough not to go back and instead hot-footed it out of the building: one of Russell's favourite tricks on his co-workers had been to imitate the cries of a helpless woman or child in order to get them to rush over to help, only to laugh at them for being tricked.

Vermeer spoke about seeing five ghostly figures walking down the back stairs as well as a night when he continued to hear footsteps coming from the floor above him, but whenever he went upstairs nobody was there, and the lights, which had previously been turned off, were back on again.

One time, Vermeer was working in the basement mopping the floor when suddenly he wasn't able to move the mop. "It was like someone was standing on it," he said. He then asked the invisible entity to get off his mop. The mop became unstuck and he then finished the job "real quick!"

Both Vermeer and Lessard have heard strange whistling echoing through the empty halls of the school and have admitted to just getting the willies for no reason at all, becoming filled with an intense desire to just get out.[13]

Several years after Suzanne's article ran in the *Spectator*, a woman named Kay submitted a story to the folks at *Haunted Hamilton* about a time when she was walking her dog in the field across the street from the school. She took a break to sit under her favourite tree when she experienced the strange feeling of being watched. Her dog started barking at the lights of a third-floor window, which were on and off; she had to struggle to pull the dog away as she slowly backed away down the street. She was convinced it was the ghost of Russell calling out to her and her pet.[14]

In 2000 a security guard, who wished to remain anonymous, described an unexplainable event that happened to him while doing a patrol during Christmas Eve.[15] He received notification that motion detectors to the office and one of the hallways were going off in the building. Responding to the call involved doing a perimeter search, then entering at the back of the parking lot and heading past the caretaker's office to the boiler room area, where the alarm could be reset.

This particular time, the guard felt a little unnerved as he descended the half-flight of stairs into the dark basement. He passed the closed caretaker's door, turned the alarms off, and then headed back upstairs to investigate the hallway, where the alarm had been activated. Finding nothing there and quickly writing up a report, he headed back downstairs to re-arm the system.

As he passed the caretaker's office, the door shot open to the sound of a radio blaring inside. He jumped and swung into the room, believing he'd found the trespassers, but nobody was inside. A moment later, as he was heading back to the boiler room, he noticed a fire door hanging open directly across from the alarm room. He shone his flashlight into the room, which was a basement gym, and found an Indian rubber ball bouncing on its own in the corner.

Understandably, he didn't stick around long. Later that evening, when he bumped into a police officer at a local Tim Hortons, the officer shared similar stories he had heard, including another officer seeing the phantom image of a little girl holding out her hand, as if to plead for help, then disappearing. He also spoke of doors opening on their own, as if some invisible gentleman were being polite to people passing through.

As mentioned earlier, the building's use as school ended in 2007. Around that time, a group of concerned residents led by Julia Kollek and calling themselves Dundas District Innovation Group put forth business plans to try to keep the school open and operating as a community arts and youth centre. There was also a lot of talk of various institutions and agencies purchasing the building. At that point, Charles Fisher, son of Robert Fisher, began a case regarding a 1989 court ruling that removed the original protective covenant of the use of the grounds for a school or public playground property. Heated debates raged on while Hamilton police continued to report break-ins, vandalism, and mischief at the abandoned building.[16]

In 2009 Mike Valvasori, a developer, and his brother Dave, bought the school for $600,000 and began the process of converting it into condos by gutting the interior and creating lofts.[17]

Strangely enough, in June 2011, a forty-five-year-old photographer who was taking pictures of the development building plunged twenty-five feet from an illegally placed construction lift. He had set up the lift to take pictures of the school from across the street and the stabilizing legs were not properly extended. The lift tipped, dumping the photographer out. He was treated on site for head injuries and rushed to the general hospital in serious but stable condition.[18]

It seems to have been an accident caused, perhaps, by a careless act. But, given the history of the Dundas school and the long history of supernatural pranks, one might have second thoughts or doubts about the cause. Could the restless spirits, perhaps eager to put a stop to the forthcoming construction, be trying to throw a proverbial "monkey wrench" into the plans? You never know.

According to the proposed construction plans, the building, or at least the core structure of it as it was originally designed, will still stand, and if plans go ahead, a new series of tenants will occupy the building.

One wonders, however, how long it might be before the new tenants begin to experience strange bumps in the night, unexplainable occurrences, and more of the otherworldly encounters so often reported on these allegedly haunted grounds.

CHAPTER THIRTEEN

THE HAMILTON ARMOURIES

In 1861 Canada didn't have any armed forces and relied on Britain to provide military protection. However, militia units have existed for most of our country's history. These units were formed from able-bodied men who were recruited locally to defend against potential rebellion or invasion. Units were formed across the country and officers were chosen from the local elite. They were called together once per year, so that the military could quickly calculate how many men might be available should a military emergency occur.[1]

The Royal Hamilton Light Infantry descends from the 13th Battalion of Volunteer Militia, which was formed in 1862 on a general order issued by the governor general. In April 1865, Hamilton's 13th Battalion of Volunteer Militia was sent to Fort Erie to defend against a frontier invasion by the Fenians.[2]

By March of 1866, Hamilton's militia still didn't have its own home. Men were stationed in drill and artillery sheds while the officers were guard mounted daily at the Mountain View Hotel.[3] In 1871, British garrisons in Canada were replaced by a newly formed Permanent Active Militia, which was composed of only two batteries of artillery, but later expanded to include cavalry and infantry.[4]

Courtesy of Stephanie Lechniak

Apparitions of old soldiers and other eerie presences can be seen and felt in the historic Hamilton Armoury.

It wasn't until 1906 that it was decided Hamilton needed to build a proper facility for the training of its militia units. After much debate and disagreements, the City of Hamilton granted a portion of land located on James Street North at Cannon for this purpose. Joseph Michael Pigott — who was also later known for the design of Hamilton City Hall, the Royal Ontario Museum, Westdale High School, and the original McMaster University buildings — designed the Hamilton Armouries. Building began in 1906 and took a full two years to complete. It was constructed entirely by men from Hamilton, one of the unique elements of its construction.[5]

The James Street Armoury, as it was originally known, was later renamed the John W. Foote VC Armoury in memory of Honorary Lieutenant-Colonel John Weir Foote, VC, CD, who, at Dieppe on August 19, 1942, was regimental chaplain with the Royal Hamilton Light Infantry. He is the only member of the Canadian Chaplain Services ever to be awarded the Victoria Cross.[6]

Foote's citation, from *The London Gazette*, February 14, 1946, reads:

> Upon landing on the beach under heavy fire he attached himself to the Regimental Aid Post which had been set up in a slight depression on the beach, but which was only sufficient to give cover to men lying down. During the subsequent period of approximately eight hours, while the action continued, this officer not only assisted the Regimental Medical Officer in ministering to the wounded in the Regimental Aid Post, but time and again left this shelter to inject morphine, give first-aid and carry wounded personnel from the open beach to the Regimental Aid Post. On these occasions, with utter disregard for his personal safety, Honorary Captain Foote exposed himself to an inferno of fire and saved many lives by his gallant efforts.
>
> During the action, as the tide went out, the Regimental Aid Post was moved to the shelter of a stranded landing craft. Honorary Captain Foote continued tirelessly and courageously to carry wounded men from the exposed beach to the cover of the landing craft. He also removed wounded from inside the landing craft when ammunition had been set on fire by enemy shells. When landing craft appeared he carried wounded from the Regimental Aid Post to the landing craft through heavy fire. On several occasions this officer had the opportunity to embark but returned to the beach as his chief concern was the care and evacuation of the

wounded. He refused a final opportunity to leave the shore, choosing to suffer the fate of the men he had ministered to for over three years.[7]

Honorary Captain Foote personally saved many lives by his efforts and his example inspired all around him. Those who observed him state that the calmness of this heroic officer as he walked about, collecting the wounded on the fire-swept beach will never be forgotten.[8]

The armouries, as they were originally designed and built, and as they stand today, are a fine reminder of Hamilton's involvement in the events that shaped this country. On the site of this beautiful landmark — one of the many locations of historic importance in Hamilton — a year-round museum exists with the purpose of acquiring, appraising, cataloguing, restoring, preserving, and displaying a collection of civilian and military artifacts important to the history of the regiment, the community, and the Canadian Forces.

What's more, according to reports provided to Haunted Hamilton, it is this particular area of the building that seems to be occupied with angry spirits.

The spirits seem to not want anybody to enter the museum. Besides weird sounds and voices being heard, particularly in the dark of night, dark shadows have been spotted flitting about out of the corner of the beholder's eye. The spirits supposedly make their presence felt in such a strong way that people feel as if they are physically being pushed out of the room.

On one occasion, a couple was visiting the museum during regular opening hours, when they walked in to see two distinct spirits materialize out of thin air and tell the woman that she simply was not welcome there. They spoke in angry and intimidating tones. Upon receiving this message, the couple turned, immediately left, and have never returned since. One wonders why the spirits might be so adamant about not wanting people to enter the room. Could they be protective of one or more of the cherished relics housed there?

In 1984 the mummified remains of a cat, now known as Victor the Regimental Cat, were found in the building. The feline's body was put on display in the museum, with an accompanying note:

> As the new drill hall neared completion a small grey alley cat cautiously inched his way along planks and up rickety wooden ladders ... As the cat neared the upper most section of the drill hall known as the flag tower, he stopped to nibble on left over sandwiches left by the workmen earlier ... After consuming the goodies, the little cat of no fixed address squeezed in between the heavy oak floor joists to escape the heat of the summer ...
>
> Alas, the workmen approached to finish off the flooring ... and poor Victor was licked under the floor, not to reappear for ninety eight years ... In the Fall of 1984 members of his regiment saw fit to remove his parched and greyed remains to a safer and more dignified location.... True to the motto "Semper Paratus" (always ready), this little soldier never left his post in the tower for almost a century....[9]

As legend has it, Victor's ghost is sometimes seen wandering the hallways at night, perhaps stalking real or spirit mice in his unearthly existence.

Several members of the Royal Hamilton Light Infantry have also insisted there are other four-legged spirits there. They're talking about the ghostly sounds and presence often experienced in the one corner where the old stables and gun sheds used to stand. The spirits of the dead horses have never been seen, but their chains and harnesses have been heard, as have the stamping of their hooves. The unmistakable and inexplicable odour of the horses has also been detected.

One story involves a group of training recruits waking in the middle of the night to the sounds of heavy breathing and the clinking of chains. One of the men cast a flashlight beam across the room, which was filled with the distinct sounds and smell of horses, and yet the beam of the light revealed nothing.

Apparently sergeants — and sergeants only — can hear the ghostly barks of a drill sergeant believed to be from the 13th Battalion, and a few have even seen him. The reason for that belief is that the drill calls can be heard on the parade square, a place that would have been the first wooden armories on that site, which burned in 1886. Sergeant Pat McCarthy created a composite illustration of the uniform worn by this particular otherworldly drill sergeant, perfectly capturing the image that was reported to have repeatedly been seen.

Another ghost appears perhaps once every couple of months and is seen walking down an old wrought-iron spiral staircase that leads to the second floor from the third floor offices. His uniform, with spiked helmet, has been identified as one worn in 1882.

Yet another ghost has been spied prowling around in the basement. One night, a guard doing a midnight patrol found the only door to a basement room unlocked. He entered and swept his flashlight across the darkness, catching sight of a man in full battledress moving around between the pillars. He called out and ran toward the intruder, but when he got closer, he realized that nobody was there.

Semi-transparent soldiers have also been seen on a particular set of balconies during parades going down James Street North. Witnesses describe seeing the spirits standing still, in full uniform, and seemingly pleased with the passing troops before fading from sight. The balconies, of course, have been reported as locked, closed off, and not used for years.[10]

If the mission statement of the Museum of the Royal Hamilton Light Infantry is to familiarize and inspire young Canadians with a history of the regiment and its part in the development of Upper Canada, then perhaps the ghosts that reside there are sentries with a similar duty, lingering out of a dedication to the preservation of a history that goes far beyond this mortal world.

CHAPTER FOURTEEN

THE WATERDOWN GHOST

In 1934 Canada had already suffered through five years of the Great Depression, evolving from being among the world's fastest growing economies to suffering an unemployment rate of almost 30 percent and a gross national product decline of 40 percent.[1]

At the start of the Great Depression, Canada's economy was shifting from primary industries, such as mining, logging, farming, and fishing, toward manufacturing. Hamilton was among the hardest hit cities, as the effect felt across the country was intensified in Canada's largest steel-manufacturing city.

Though a slightly strengthening economy was met in the summer of 1934 with a severe drought that destroyed crops and injected further hardships into an already stressed society, not all the talk in Waterdown was about the economy or the weather.[2]

More often than not, as people met on street corners or shared gossip with one another over the fences in their backyards, there was much discussion regarding a strange, unknown figure seen about town.

The village of Waterdown, which since 2001 has been amalgamated into the city of Hamilton, was established on the edge of the Niagara Escarpment, east of the junction of King's Highways

5 and 6. Legend holds that the name of the community stems from Ebenezer Culver Griffin, who purchased a portion of land from Alexander Brown in 1823 and a dozen years later had it surveyed into village lots. Griffin was a prohibitionist who disapproved of the vast quantities of alcohol being consumed, particularly during the christening of new mills. A spectator shouting out, "Hey Ebenezer, throw that water down!" while a carpenter was christening a mill led to it being known as Waterdown, which was then adopted as the name for the village itself.[3]

As described in an article entitled "The Walking Wraith of Waterdown," published by *The Waterdown–East Flamborough Heritage Society*, Art Hood and his family were driving home from church one Sunday night when they first spotted a stranger, unfamiliar to his family, dressed completely in white, standing on the side of the road. But it wasn't until Hood saw the man again that he contacted the local police to inquire about him. The police could find no evidence of such a man living in Waterdown.[4]

Nonetheless, reports began to stream in from others spotting him in similar situations, and suddenly there was talk everywhere of the strange man in white appearing in outlying concessions as well as in town.

Nervous whispers that flowed through the community described the white stranger as being very tall (with some accounts putting him at over seven feet) with humongous feet. Footprints left in the dust where he was spotted reportedly measured several inches beyond the largest shoe size commonly available at that time in the community.

Known as the "Walking Wraith," the strange visitor was most often seen at night along the fourth concession. Couples parked in cars along the side of the road for some privacy were often the targets of this stranger's advances. Their nighttime sessions of romance became evenings of terror, the lovers crying out not in passion but fear when the wraith suddenly appeared, approaching the vehicle through the fog-like dust of the side of the road.[5]

Thankfully, nobody was injured or killed in any of these alleged sightings — with the exception, perhaps, of a shrieking and terrified female clawing at her companion, yelling for him to start the car.

Perhaps in an unintended ode to Waterdown founder Ebenezer Griffin's prohibitionist attitude, an abrupt end came to the young couples' vehicular necking sessions. But children and women were also kept close to home and inside after dark as a wave of mass panic continued to spread throughout the town.

Those with a bit more courage and bravado scoured the area when the sun went down, hoping to capture or trap the wraith, and newspaper accounts began to appear in the local papers as well as in Toronto. The village very quickly began to attract visitors who were hoping to spy the Waterdown Wraith for themselves. Roads were reported to have been filled to capacity with people flocking in from outlying communities, likely as eager to catch a glimpse of the spectre as they were to escape the day-to-day angst of the Depression and drought.

Most newshounds and tourists failed to satisfy their morbid curiosity, but one reporter from *The Toronto Evening Telegram* saw the apparition. The reporter bemused that, despite legends having ghosts drifting over the ground, this particular one was spied running, even stumbling through a field. What's more, when it came to a fence, instead of melting through it as ghosts are wont to do, the Waterdown Wraith climbed over it.[6]

As popular as the visions of the ghost had been in the early days of the mass paranoia, regular sightings that were obvious pranks, or copycats, began to pop up, becoming even more popular than the original. Instead of prowling after dark in search of a ghost, men were loading their shotguns and awaiting the arrival of a prankster.

A woman thinking it would be good sport to have some fun with her jittery husband decided to play a prank on him one night. Sneaking off into some bushes near the house, she waited patiently until he was walking past from an errand to fetch a milk bottle and a bucket of water. Just as he neared, she leapt from the bushes, wrapped in a white sheet, shouting, "Boo!" Fearing for his life, he reacted by knocking the "ghost" over the head with the milk bottle. Seconds after the fear abated and he could see that it was his wife, he used water from the bucket he had been carrying to revive her.[7]

Russell Thompson, a track team member and medical student from Toronto, and the Briggar boys, two well-known high-school athletes, were top suspects in the local investigations of alleged pranks due to their sprinting ability. They also lived on the fourth concession, which was a popular area for sightings of the ghost.[8]

One particular evening, members of the fire department spotted a figure dressed in white at a distance and started to follow it up the railway track and into the Thompson driveway. The next morning, when Officer Darby of the Ontario Provincial Police arrived at the Thompson house, requesting he be allowed to search for evidence of a ghost, Mr. Thompson reportedly stated that if people didn't drink so much beer, they likely wouldn't be seeing ghosts.[9]

As the summer ended, and September arrived, sightings of the ghost and the prankish behaviours also came to an end. Some attributed this to Thompson's return to medical school in Toronto, while others speculated that perhaps the original Waterdown Wraith had found what he was looking for.[10]

One wonders, though, prior to the rise of pranks and the copycat ghosts that came later, just who that original stranger dressed in white was and what he was doing wandering the sides of the roadway. Was he a wraith with some malicious intent, or merely a spirit trapped in time?

For whatever reason, Waterdown seemed to grow and expand over the following decades without any further evidence of ghostly presences, until 1978, when two tombstones were discovered at the Waterdown Library (the former East Flamborough Township Hall) as Mill Street underwent extensive renovations.

The white marble tombstones commemorating Alexander Brown and Merren Grierson (owners of one of the very first land grants in the area) hang outside the library's elevator, which has been reported to have continued to operate by itself for the better part of three decades.[11]

Over the years, other eyewitnesses have recounted similar tales. One young man was searching for a book on the second floor, when the elevator door opened for no apparent reason. Patrons would often blame these occurrences on a "crappy elevator."

Despite multiple inspections, elevator mechanics are baffled as to what could be causing the elevator to move up and down between floors, opening and closing its doors without human guidance. Visitors to the library, which was originally built in 1850, have reported not only seeing the elevator operate independently, but have also mentioned hearing unexplainable voices and footsteps.

Many people believe there is a simple and straightforward explanation for the strange occurrences: Merren Grierson haunts the library, perhaps drawn to the building by the tombstone that bears her name (or, at least, a slight misspelling of her name, since the tombstone gives her first name as "Merion").

In any case, Waterdown, a community that has grown from a small village into a vastly expanding hub for commuters from Hamilton and Toronto, has long had its share of local lore and spirits.

CHAPTER FIFTEEN

HAUNTED MCMASTER

Having worked at Titles Bookstore at McMaster between 2006 and 2011, I've had many opportunities to be on campus alone after dark, to walk the empty halls of the buildings, to be by myself in a place that, perhaps just hours before, was bustling with thousands of students, faculty, and staff members, all hurrying on their way to complete another day of their academic rounds. To me, there's always something just a bit eerie about being in a vacant location that is normally teeming with people. The unexpected quiet and calm offers an unsettling feeling.

In the course of finalizing the work on this book, in the late summer of 2011, I had worked several late nights at the campus bookstore, all in the lead-up to what is known in academia as the "September rush." Several evenings, when packing and heading out to leave, my footsteps echoing off the walls, feeling as if I were the only person in the building, perhaps even on campus, the sheer concept of isolation sent a chill down my spine. It's not unlike the chill I used to get walking through the tunnels that connect most of the older buildings on the campus at Carleton University, where I worked twenty years earlier while I was a student there.

Indeed, aren't schools themselves somewhat of a hotbed for speculation about ghosts? Isn't almost any academic hall some sort of mystical lightning rod for the generation of creepy tales?

I remember my own elementary school, Levack Public School, in Levack, Ontario, as being rumoured to have a ghost living in the basement. For weeks on end one year, my schoolmates and I would taunt one another and dare others to run inside, head down the stairs, race down the basement hall, come up the stairs on the other side of the building, and exit — *if* you made it out alive at all, of course. Because the ghost that lived down there and was sometimes heard playing the old abandoned piano that was stored at the end of the hall might get you. Naturally, many attempts were made, but few people got more than a few steps inside before hearing some thump or clack and racing back up to the door they had entered to share their wild, hot tale of terror and convince their friends they had indeed seen the ghost.

We might have grown up and escaped the games of childhood that kept us entertained during lunch break or recess, but as we moved on to buildings of higher education, we never really left those tendencies behind; perhaps because, as we learned more about the world, even as we learned about science and math and all other matters associated with reason and logic, we also embraced that feeling of reasonable doubt — the feeling that perhaps there is something out there that defies explanation, something that offers us a window into the afterlife, something that reveals to us an echo of times long past.

The research for this particular chapter began well before this book was even conceived. Since I started working at Titles, McMaster's bookstore, we began to hold a "mysterious" or "spooky" annual event in the days leading up to Halloween. One year we hosted a "Who Murdered Manager Mark" event, where customers came in to a fictional crime scene where I had reportedly been found dead. Six staff members were listed as potential suspects, and customers were invited to regularly return to check out the clues hidden throughout the store every day for a full week and fill out an investigator sheet outlining who they believed the killer might be.

The following year we hosted a group of horror authors, including Canada's John Robert Colombo, and paired up with Daniel and Stephanie from Haunted Hamilton Ghost Walks & Events. The group offered a free custom ghost walk of the campus that began and ended at the bookstore, where the authors were doing readings and signing copies of their books up until midnight.

In 2009 we again held ghost walks hosted by the folks from Haunted Hamilton, and inside the store we launched a specially themed anthology of ghost stories printed exclusively on our Espresso Book Machine. Entitled *Campus Chills*, the book featured ghost stories set on university and college campuses from across Canada. Some of the stories were based on actual legends or ghost stories familiar to the campus they were set at.

For the McMaster story, which I co-wrote with my friend, McMaster graduate Kimberly Foottit, we conceived of the ghost of a dead Shakespearean scholar who comes back to seek revenge on those who would dare replicate his precious "folio" edition of the bard's works. Our tale was a tongue-in-cheek spot of dark humour regarding a traditional and conservative academic mind clashing with the future shock of new technology. But prior to setting about to write the tale, I had done some research to see if McMaster had any ghosts of its own that could inspire our story.

Frighteningly, there was no shortage of rumours, tales, and sad events peppering the history of the campus.

I learned the horrific tale of a quiet December evening when a history professor was working alone in her office, and a transient stranger wandering the campus jumped her for unknown reasons. She was found the next day, handcuffed and asphyxiated from a rag shoved too far into her mouth and throat.

Universities like McMaster inspire both learning and eerie legends.

There were also, unfortunately, many sad accounts of women who were brutally slain or murdered, sometimes after being grabbed by a stranger while walking on campus after dark, but more often by a boyfriend or an ex-boyfriend whose grief, anger, and feelings of helplessness led him down a shockingly horrific path that would end the life of a young woman in the prime of her youth.

Out of respect for those who had relatively recently died at McMaster, Kim and I decided to stick with our completely fictitious tale. We preferred the concept of an outraged dead scholar lurking in the shadows of the library and bookstore, killing off those who dared replicate and thus soil the sacred text he so cherished.

Similarly, this book is not the place to share those tragic tales.

However, McMaster University, given its long history, is no stranger to ghostly tales, and many continue to keep residence students awake long into the night, or provide reasons for a person walking alone down the deserted hallway of a one-hundred-year-old building to question the odd shadows seen out of the corner of the eye.

The main campus of McMaster University is located on almost four-hundred acres of land in the Westdale neighbourhood, adjacent to the Royal Botanical Gardens and bordered to the north by Cootes Paradise, an extensive natural marshland.[1]

The institution bears the name of William McMaster, a prominent Canadian senator who bequeathed just under one million dollars toward the founding of the university, which was the result of the merger of Toronto Baptist College and Woodstock College.

McMaster first opened in Toronto, Ontario, in 1890. However, inadequate lands and a huge campaign and donation of land by the City of Hamilton prompted the university to relocate to Hamilton in 1930.[2]

The very first ghost story associated with McMaster is related to the founder of the institution rather than its location in Hamilton, but the tale itself is one worthy to be shared, particularly for those looking for an eerie romp.

In 1867 the McMaster family built the mansion that still stands at 515 Jarvis Street West, in Toronto. Arthur McMaster, nephew to the founder of McMaster University, was its first owner. In 1880 the house was purchased by the Massey family and renamed Euclid Hall. (The Massey family would be associated with Toronto's Massey Hall among other significant landmarks.)[3]

Euclid Hall was given to Victoria College in 1915, and the

building served as a radio station, an art gallery, and a restaurant before being purchased by The Keg in 1976.[4]

The mansion is reportedly haunted by various different ghosts. The first of which is the maid of Lillian Massey. Lillian, who was the only daughter of Hart Massey, was beloved by family and staff alike. Legend has it that, upon her death in 1915, the maid was so distraught that she took her own life by means of a noose attached to the oval vestibule above the main staircase. The ghost is sometimes seen hanging in this very same spot.[5]

The phantom footsteps of children can sometimes be heard from the second floor, which used to be the children's quarters. The ghost of a young boy is seen running up and down the stairs and occasionally sitting at the top and watching diners in the restaurant below.[6]

The women's washroom is also said to be haunted by an unseen but strongly felt presence. There are reports of feeling the cold chill of being watched when alone in the washroom, the lock on their stall coming unlocked on its own, and even a fallen handbag slowly drifting to the floor, as if being guided there by unseen hands.[7]

So begin the creepy tales that speak of the history one might find when walking the halls of the oldest buildings at McMaster. And the next story, while closer to campus, is still in a separate location; it involves a building owned by McMaster that is located right in the heart of Hamilton's downtown.

Known by McMaster insiders as DTC, the Downtown Centre — the building at 50 Main Street West — is the home of various offices such as payroll, accounts payable, and the centre for continuing education. Other entities also exist in this building.

And these are ones who don't pay for tuition or occupy a solid space — at least not for long.

The building used to be home to the Wentworth County Courthouse, and, over the years, many people have reported hearing, seeing, and feeling strange things in the area where some jail cells still remain. Some claim, working in the building after hours, that they have had the uncanny feeling of being watched and even caught glimpses of shadowy figures out of the corner of their eyes, down a corridor that they raced toward only to find empty.

Others claim to have heard voices coming from adjacent vacant rooms while working on a Saturday, a time when most of the building is completely unoccupied.

When wondering about the possibility of ghosts, and the fact that the building used to be a courthouse and jail, one wonders if perhaps executions might have taken place there, offering some sort of reason behind the strange noises and frightening shadows.

But the closest historical records come to supporting such a theory would be the public executions which took place back in the 1890s at gallows facing Jackson Street at the rear of 50 Main Street West. Is it close enough for the misguided spirits to continue to linger and make their presence felt? You might just ask one of the employees of the Downtown Centre at McMaster who has experienced the unexplainable sights and sounds.

So far we've taken a bit of a stroll around the periphery, through history related to McMaster and to one of the "outpost" locations — but what about the main campus itself? Sure, McMaster residence life can lay claim to having a part in inspiring *Animal House* director Ivan Reitman, but might it also lay claim to inspiring tales from the shadows?

Well, there's always Anthony B. Percy, the resident ghost at Wallingford Hall.

This ghost tale has its start in 1934. Back then, there were two residences on campus. Edwards Hall, an all-male dorm, and Wallingford Hall, for females. Anthony Percy and Mary Baxter had the chance, through various social activities between the two residences, to get to know each other and become friends. They would spend leisurely afternoons in the Wallingford Tea Room or the Gentleman's Waiting Area (two of the only places males were allowed to venture in the all-female building).

Courtesy of Peter Rainford.

University Hall at McMaster boasts a Collegiate Gothic design with unique carved mouldings in the entranceways.

As time passed, Mary became rather fond of Anthony. She found herself slowly and inevitably falling in love with him. This love mutated rather quickly into an obsession. As their moments of spending long segments of time started to fade away, and Anthony would engage in activities with other people, Mary found herself seeking him out. No matter where he went on campus, she was often not far behind, attempting to keep him in her sights. She was even occasionally spotted outside his room at night, quietly standing and simply looking in his window at him while he studied.

Anthony, however, was oblivious to Mary's feelings for him. To him, she was a friend, someone whom he enjoyed spending time with. And unbeknownst to Mary, Anthony's heart had already begun the process of belonging completely to another woman. It thus came as quite the shock to Mary when she found out that the love of her life had become engaged to another woman.

Shortly after she found this out, Mary requested a meeting with him in the Wallingford Tea Room, the place where they'd spend so many lovely and contented afternoons together, and where Mary had slowly fallen in love with this man of her dreams, this man who had betrayed her and broken her heart.

When Anthony arrived, Mary confessed her true feelings to him as well as her anger at his betrayal. Their conversation devolved rather quickly into a heated argument. The argument apparently ended with the sound of a loud thud coming from the tea room. A few minutes later, by the time someone entered the room to investigate the noise and the abruptly ended argument, the room was empty.

Anthony's body was found stuffed in the dumbwaiter, and Mary was nowhere to be found.[8] To this day, the whereabouts of Mary Baxter is a complete mystery; however, if you ask certain people who have stayed in Wallingford Hall, they might tell you they know exactly where Anthony B. Percy is.

He is still there. Ironically, a man who was never allowed to venture far into Wallingford Hall now haunts the building for the rest of eternity.

Over the years, various stories have been shared regarding strange incidents that are sometimes attributed to the ghost of Anthony. Closed windows are found propped open, shower curtains have been pulled back and forth, lights are said to turn on and off by themselves, and, occasionally, a low and quiet weeping can be heard echoing off the washroom walls when there is nobody inside.

Of course, the tales of Mary Baxter and Anthony B. Percy might just be a story born of an evening of high spirits, with one or more residents wanting to create a tale to put a fun scare into the other people there. And this story might just be one of those fictions passed down through many generations of Wallingford Hall residents.

However, if you're one of the students living in the old building and you experience the strange sensation of a blanket being pulled off, a shadow flitting past, or the odd sounds of crying from a vacant adjacent room, it might be a little harder, in the chill of the moment, to chalk it all up to an old myth that grew out of hand.

CHAPTER SIXTEEN

THE TIVOLI THEATRE

One would well expect a theatre to be filled with the voices of actors, the patter of footsteps treading the boards of the stage, and fantastical images inspired by the imagination of playwrights and directors. But the old Tivoli Theatre in Hamilton offered those things even when supposedly quiet and between performances, sending a quick shiver of fright up the spines of employees and actors who worked there.

Many looked at the remains of the Tivoli Theatre building as a forgotten ruin of an era long past. The 750-seat auditorium still stands vacant, but in 2004, when a portion of the south wall facing James Street North (the area containing the lobby, office space, washrooms, props room and storage space) began to collapse, it was deemed unsafe, and the demolition of that entire section began.

The Tivoli was built in three sections; the first section was constructed in 1875. The section that used to front James Street North was built with a carriage factory on the upper floors and retail shops at street level. The architecture of the building has been described as a Second Empire style, boasting a steeply pitched mansard roof with dormers, bracketed cornices, and rich classical detailing.

For almost one hundred years, the Tivoli Theatre buildings were the centre for entertainment in the city of Hamilton.

The carriage factory closed in 1881 and the building remained vacant until 1907, when the theatre community in Hamilton began to rise. The factory was converted to a theatre with about two hundred seats, and Hamilton city records reveal that in 1908 a theatre known as the Wonderland opened on the site at the rear of the factory building, showing live vaudeville acts. In 1909 it was renamed the Colonial and in 1913 the name changed once more to The Princess at about the same time it began showing motion pictures.[1]

A theatre magnate of the 1900s named Ambrose Small owned the Tivoli (The Princess at that point) along with several other theatres in Southern Ontario. In 1919 he signed a contract selling all of his theatres — The Tivoli in Hamilton, The Grand in London, and The Grand in Toronto — for a couple million dollars. But on the fateful and sunny afternoon of Friday, December 19, Small walked away from a pleasant meeting with his lawyer FWM Flock on the corner of Adelaide and Yonge in Toronto and was never seen again.[2, 3]

Small's disappearance became one of the most captivating and enduring mysteries of the time. He was not only a theatre mogul but also a ruthless businessman, a gambler, and an adulterous rogue. He openly hated children, the less fortunate, and regularly complained that his wife's benevolent nature and participation in charities was a waste of time.

Small's ruthless nature amplified the hype surrounding his bizarre disappearance and sent the media into a tailspin, as might happen with more modern celebrities, who shine in the spotlight merely because of the way that people love to hate them,

A $50,000 reward was offered for anyone finding Ambrose Small alive, and $15,000 was offered if his dead body was recovered. A stream of claims poured in, with many of the dead bodies closely fitting Small's appearance. But each of them was disproved by a single fact that was held from the public's knowledge: Small had hammertoes.[4]

On the same day that Small went missing, his long-time assistant, John Doughty, also went missing. Doughty, however, was reportedly seen in Montreal the following day, and almost a year later was captured and questioned by police in Oregon while living under a false name. And though he was found to not be guilty of Small's disappearance, Doughty was found guilty of stealing $104,000 in bonds that had belonged to his boss.[5]

The last place Small was seen was in his office in The Grand Theatre in Toronto, but a stream of eyewitness accounts three quarters of a century after he disappeared suggest that though Small's physical body was never seen again, his spirit has returned to the Hamilton theatre that he owned.

In 1924 the old carriage factory was converted into a lobby and the back part of the structure was rebuilt into a bold new auditorium to impress patrons and compete with the Capital, Hamilton's crown jewel of theatres at the time.[6]

In 1926 it was the theatre that brought "talkies" to Hamilton and was perhaps one of the very first in Canada to do so.

In 1954, Famous Players spent $250,000 in renovations on the auditorium, reworking the previous Italian Renaissance theme and installing special lighting effects. One of the other major renovations involved converting the balcony into a smoking area. Throughout the 1940s and 1950s, smoking became an extremely popular activity, particularly since it was featured regularly in movies and partaken in by all of the coolest roles played by the most well-loved actors of the day.

In September 1989, Famous Players closed the theatre down, with the last show being *Indiana Jones and the Last Crusade*. That same year, Sam Sniderman bought the building for $1.7 million, converting the front area into a record store (a Hamilton location for his popular *Sam the Record Man* chain). Famous Players made Sniderman sign a contract with a clause stating that, while he could put on musical acts and stage plays there, he was not able to show a movie there for twenty years.

In 1991, playwright Douglas Rodger's *How Could You, Mrs. Dick?* was put on by Theatre Terra Nova and drew in massive crowds, a reminder of the days in which the beautiful seductress drew crowds of spectators to the trial in which she was accused of murdering her husband, John Dick.

This is about the time that, after more than seventy-two years, Ambrose Small was again spotted. Was this the ghost of the theatre magnate making a suggestion regarding his own wife Theresa's involvement in his disappearance, or merely a coincidence?

Loren Lieberman was the manager of the theatre at this time and, soon after he and his crew moved in, was continually approached by both staff and actors who claimed to see an apparition of a man in various locations throughout the building. Describing the ghost as looking like he was homeless, but not in contemporary clothes of the time, instead wearing a more Victorian style of dress, they noted he bore a single striking feature: a long curled moustache like the one that Salvador Dali was known for.

Lieberman went to the Hamilton Public Library and picked up a book that contained pictures of Small. When he showed the staff the pictures of the theatre magnate, one by one, they each independently agreed that this was the man they had spotted wandering the theatre.

Many renovations took place during this time, and that was when a secret basement location containing many old vaudeville posters, movie reels, and steamer trunks was found. One trunk had a gold plate on the front with A. SMALL carved into it. When the workers opened it, they at first thought they had discovered a theatre prop of a skeleton, but upon closer inspection, the bones inside were real.

Lieberman called the Toronto police (the closest forensics team at the time), informing them of the find and the potential that this might be the remains of the long-lost theatre mogul. The police team was scheduled to arrive the next day. However, renovation-related confusion led to the trunk's disappearance before they arrived; nobody is sure whether the trunk was tossed out with so much of the rubbish or if it disappeared under more suspicious circumstances. The A. SMALL trunk's ultimate destiny also remains a mystery.

But if Small's ghost haunts the theatre, he is certainly not alone.

A spirit that was seen most often at the Tivoli is a woman in a long 1920s dress. Seen by many employees and actors over the years, this shy ghost would disappear rather quickly whenever she was spotted by the living. This act made her appearances that much more unsettling and memorable for those who spied her.

Lieberman, who, as manager, had spent more time in the theatre than any of the actors or employees, was frustrated that the woman had quickly shown herself to virtually everybody except for him. He had even joked about being the one person left out, until one day he and a female employee were engaged in a conversation, when she looked away from Lieberman in mid sentence and went completely pale.

Turning to see what the employee was looking at, Lieberman saw the woman standing directly behind him. It appeared as if she were trying to frantically tell him something, but though her lips were moving, neither Lieberman nor the employee could hear a thing. They both could distinctly make out that she was saying his name, Loren, over and over before she faded from sight.

Another occurrence that Lieberman himself never experienced, but which he had heard multiple accounts of, was of patrons using the restrooms off the lobby and hearing voices all around them on their walk back to the auditorium. They said that though the lobby was empty, there were sounds as if a large crowd were mingling there.

Lieberman had one dedicated worker of the canine variety, a Rottweiler he named Norbert T. Rottweiler, or Nobby for short. Nobby patrolled the lobby and foyer at night, ensuring that this building, which wasn't in the best of the downtown neighbourhoods, would remain secure from break-ins.

One morning when Lieberman arrived at the theatre, he discovered that Nobby was missing. The dog was nowhere to be found in either the foyer or the lobby. Hearing a soft whimpering from behind his office door, Lieberman unlocked it and found Nobby inside.

Confused as to how a dog could have gotten through a locked door in the middle of the night, Lieberman and some employees reviewed the security footage. They watched in shocked fascination as the locked office door opened by itself to let the dog inside, then slammed shut behind Nobby.

This happened on more than one night, confusing and frustrating Lieberman. Determined to try to solve the mystery, Lieberman and a group of employees lingered in the lobby in the middle of the night, directly across from the locked office. When Lieberman prompted Nobby to go into his office, the dog walked up to the door and put his paw on it. The door suddenly swung open long enough for the dog to walk in, then it abruptly closed again.

The witnessing group was dumbfounded.

Lieberman walked up to the door, placed his hand on it, and gave a little push. It didn't budge. He then threw his entire two hundred pounds against the door, but still it didn't budge. The door didn't in fact open until he took out the keys and unlocked it.

That particular occurrence eventually stopped happening after just a few more confusing and eerie nights, but there was yet more to fear.

Under the statue of Caesar on the south side of the auditorium lurks the distressed spirit of a young boy who is regularly heard but not often seen. Several staff and patrons who heard a faint weeping rushed to the large vent under the statue and tore it off the wall, thinking to rescue the boy they thought was hopelessly trapped within. But there was nobody inside to rescue — except perhaps for a ghost, for whom it is too late to save. One rather curious witness to the crying went so far as to crawl inside the dusty vent, discovering a report card belonging to a local Hamilton boy from Ryerson elementary school's grade 4.[7]

In the summer of 2002, the folks at Haunted Hamilton conducted an investigation of the Tivoli Theatre. Their psychics went into the building without being told any of the alleged history of the ghosts. Immediately drawn to the statue and the vent, they placed their hands on the wall and said it housed an important document.

Shortly after a side wall collapsed in upon itself in 2004, leaving a gaping hole on the south side of the building, city contractors assessed the structure as unstable. The City of Hamilton billed owner Sam Sniderman $300,000 for the cost of the demolition.

Courtesy of Stephanie Lechniak

Legends suggest that the distressed spirit of a young boy lurks near the statue of Caesar on the south side of the auditorium.

In 2006 the Canadian Ballet Youth Ensemble bought the building from Sniderman for either one or two dollars, depending on which newspaper report you read. And in the summer of 2010, Gina Gintili and Belma Diamante began trying to raise five million dollars in order to restore the theatre building into a dance, arts, and culture centre. Under a campaign called "Toonies for Tivoli," they hope to build those funds two dollars at a time. They champion the Tivoli as a magic spot, larger than the real estate and a symbol of our city's soul.

Those who have experienced the unexplained occurrences at the Tivoli would, of course, also suggest that there is more than magic here — and that if the legendary building known as the Tivoli rises again, so, too, will the ghosts that continue to tread the boards there.

CHAPTER SEVENTEEN

GUS'S GHOST STORY

The following is an article that appeared in the August 16, 1902, issue of the *Hamilton Herald*. Brother's Robert B. and John M. Harris established the newspaper in August 1889, and it became Hamilton's first one-cent newspaper, making Hamilton into a three-newspaper town. The *Hamilton Spectator*, started in 1846, and the *Hamilton Times*, 1859, were the other two papers at the time — the only remaining daily newspaper today is the *Spectator*. The *Herald* lasted until 1936; the *Times* until 1920.

Interestingly, parts of the story, namely the pulling of bedclothes, appeared in other accounts of ghostly occurrences reported by both men and women. What I couldn't determine is if these other tales were related to this original haunting experience that Nelson reports.

His Weird Experience with Tricky Spook
The House Is Said to Be Haunted

Whether or not you believe in the truth of the following story, told by Gus Nelson, of this town, it is certain that the teller of the story is convinced of its truth. As he told it to a small group of friends one evening this week, he had not fully recovered from the nerve-shaking effects of his experience. He said:

"On the night of Wednesday, August 6, I went to bed in my boarding house on Park Street about half-past ten. Not being tired or sleepy, I lay for some time in deep thought. Suddenly, I was disturbed by a curious, weird sound, as if made by the rattling of chains or someone trying to open the door. This noise increased, and was followed by a louder sound, as of someone hitting the head of an empty barrel with a mallet. Being slightly alarmed, I sat up in bed and called out, 'Get to the dickens out of this,' though I could see nothing. Presently, as if by magic, a light appeared in the hallway, which just as suddenly disappeared again. Then I felt something pulling at the bed clothes. Reaching under the bed I seized a slipper and fired it at the apparition. Scarcely had I lain down again before the clothes again moved. I grasped them tightly, but the ghost also pulled. For a time it was difficult to tell which would gain the mastery. Again the light appeared and the pulling ceased. For a long time I lay in a state of bewilderment and great fatigue. I fell asleep. I awoke, with a feeling of nervousness, about 4:30 a.m. I looked, and there was the light again. It came and went at intervals, positively without human agency. Upon recovering myself sufficiently afterwards, I found a pair of old socks on top of my head and the bed clothes lying in the center of the room on the floor."

In the group of persons to whom Gus told his story was Night Watchman Jamieson, who is well known to be an authority on ghosts and several other important matters. Mr. Jamieson exhibited no surprise over the story. The house, he said, had been haunted for some time, that condition having been brought about by the fact that a man had hung himself there some seven years ago. Ever since then the apparition of a man had occasionally been seen walking about at midnight sometimes with a small electric light in one hand and sometimes pounding on an empty barrel with a drumstick. One night, says Jamieson, a policeman saw the apparition. He immediately fainted and was restored to consciousness by Jamieson himself. The next night the policeman was not on that beat, and it was reported that he was sick.

Gus Nelson says that a young man who had slept there before he came said the bed actually walked over to the door, and that such things as Gus described were of common occurrence. To say that, Gus, who was [illegible] frightened is but mildly expressing it, and money could not induce him to return to his boarding house, as he is quite positive that it was a ghost he saw. No one can make him believe different. A certain gentleman to whom Gus was relating his experience, says that he had often been visited by ghosts, and that the only way to get rid of them was to stand a bottle of whisky and a glass in front of the bed. They would then take a drink and depart without touching the bed clothes. This is about the best remedy I have ever heard of to banish ghosts, and if any ever bother me I think I shall take this means of disposing them.

CHAPTER EIGHTEEN

THE TOMBSTONE GHOST

On an otherwise typical Sunday night in June 1971, around the time that Ontario Place opened in Toronto, Federal Express was founded in Little Rock, Arkansas, and *The Ed Sullivan Show* made its last broadcast on CBS-TV, Norm and Sherrie Bilotti encountered something dark and mysterious in their home — a far more memorable event for them.

Norm Bilotti was startled out of a peaceful midsummer night's dream by the shrill screams of his wife, Sherrie. When his eyes shot open, he immediately spied what was causing Sherrie's sudden bout of night terrors: a faceless female shape cloaked in a long flowing gown was hovering just a few feet above their bed. They were both frozen in fear, staring at the figure before them and trying to determine exactly what it was.

Norm vocalized his query, asking his wife what the hell it was as he sat up in the bed. Almost as if in reaction to his voice and motion, the shape slowly moved to the foot of the bed. He was able to estimate her height as approximately six feet before it retreated from the bed and toward the wall. It seemed to grow smaller, then completely vanished.

Not believing his eyes, Norm leapt from the bed, ran to

the light switch, and lit up the room. There was nothing by the wall where the figure had disappeared. He moved to other rooms of the house, switching on lights as he went. Again, there was nothing. He continued to check the rest of their ground-floor apartment as well as the yard outside and could find no indication that anyone had entered their apartment.

However this intruder had entered their home, she certainly hadn't come in through a door or window.

Sherrie explained to her husband that she had felt something behind her, looking at her, and when she opened her eyes, she spotted the figure hovering above her head — that is when she started screaming in terror.

Norm did not believe in ghosts. He admitted that if it had been either of them alone who had seen the spectre, they could have easily passed it off as something they had imagined, or perhaps a brief moment of hysterical insanity. But the fact that they both saw it made them all the more curious.

Ever the scientific mind, not willing to entertain the notion of ghosts, Norm stated that he wanted to see it again in order to understand what it really was. Sherrie, on the other hand, had trouble sleeping without leaving some sort of light on; a habit she continued for a good three weeks after this event.

Twenty-eight days after their first encounter with the ghost, she appeared again.

This time it was Norm who was first woken from his sleep, not by a sound but by the overwhelming feeling of being watched. When he opened his eyes he saw the figure hovering above the bed. Again, it was roughly the size of a woman and draped in flowing robes. But this time the figure's face and features came into focus. Her face had bulging eyes and hair standing straight up as if it had been charged with electricity.

"Do you see it?" Norm called out to his wife.

She responded that she had and remarked about the hair standing on end.

As Norm surveyed the figure in more detail, noticing it was different from the last time, he observed that it only had half a body. Just the top half of its torso was floating above them.

One of them screamed, likely unable to contain the mounting terror building inside them, and the creature quickly withdrew from above the bed and disappeared.

Despite the fact that the apartment was right beside a graveyard, Norm still refused to believe that what they had seen was a ghost. But he did begin to learn more about the residence from neighbours.

The house they were in had been built twenty-four years earlier by the man who opened an adjacent hardware store. He lived in the house with his wife, who had been crippled and confined to a wheelchair, and their five children. The man was well-respected in the neighbourhood, and following his wife's death two years earlier, he sold the building; that is when Norm and Sherrie moved in as tenants of the new owner.

Norm worked as a compositor at the *Hamilton Spectator*, and after some discussion with colleagues at work, he and Sherrie agreed to let a reporter from the newspaper investigate. Details of the investigation were published in the *Spectator* on November 27 in a feature article called "In Search of a Ghost." Written by John Bryden, the article documented the mysterious sightings of the Bilotti family as well as the intense investigation that took place.[1]

Twenty-seven-year-old Malcolm Bessent, a professional spiritual medium, was called in. Bessent was from the Human Dimensions Institute of Rosary Hill College in Buffalo, New York. He said he had developed his psychic ability via practised discipline. He explained that he worked best when he was able to keep a calm and almost non-personal approach. If he got too close or personally involved with any of his subjects, he said that his accuracy faded; he chalked it up to emotions as being a clouding factor in the special vision he was gifted with.

Rabbi Bernard Baskin and Dr. A. S. MacPherson also agreed to participate as independent witnesses.

None of the three men involved in this investigation were told of the situation or even where the ghost had supposedly appeared, just that they were investigating an apparent haunting.

One of the first statements Bessent made when he arrived at the scene was that they were dealing with a family of four children. Given what was known at the time, his statement appeared wrong, or at least off by one. Circumstances were eventually uncovered, however, which proved his initial statement correct. The previous family had five children, but one turned out to be adopted. So, while there were five children, the woman whose spirit they believed they were seeing was the birth mother of four.

Bessent expressed his concern at how many people were present in such a small space. He explained that he was apt to receive interference from their thoughts. But when he walked into the bedroom, the situation was immediately clear to him. "There's definitely something here," was the first thing he said. Then he added that it was a woman and she was disabled.

At that point, Bessent asked that everyone except the accompanying reporter (John Bryden), the rabbi, and the doctor leave the room. When they left, he became serious, explaining that the woman had died in an extremely painful way and that he was getting a sense of a name starting with S. He suggested a name like Sam or Sarah, as well as the initials S.A. He also alluded to the fact that he kept seeing green and white flowers, and mentioned that the date 1947 was significant.

Later investigation showed that the woman's maiden name had been Flowers, that the family were active members in the Salvation Army, and that the property had been purchased in 1947. It is possible that the statements Bessent made were simple coincidence, or they might be evidence of some connection he had been making.

The next thing Bessent remarked about was that he was getting an overwhelming sense of an awful, rancid smell associated with the presence, and he commented on it several times. Sherrie Bilotti later talked about occasionally catching the whiff of an awful odour, as if something dead were in the house; only, each time they went to investigate the source (suspecting a plugged drain or some other likely cause), they couldn't determine where the smell was coming from.

Bessent also talked about hearing screaming all the time: whatever it was that was haunting this apartment was constantly screeching. Then he suggested that the ghost they had seen was very likely trying to draw their attention to something in the room, something nearby, something hidden. He became certain that there was something either in the walls or in the basement, and dragged the investigative team into the basement of the building, where he said there was something hidden there, something hidden between wood and stone.

The Bilottis knew that, as tenants and not owners of the building, they didn't have any right to be tearing up the floor and walls, so they left it at a thought and something they simply wouldn't be able to do in their search for answers.

Shortly after speculating that it would be interesting to see what might be behind the walls or under a blocked-off set of stairs, Bessent became fatigued. The investigation wrapped up for the night, and merely a few weeks later, Norm and Sherrie Bilotti moved to a new apartment.

They never saw the eerie spectre in the middle of the night again.

The story would have ended there, and in many ways it did. Norm and Sherrie went on to live a normal, peaceful existence; never again did they wake in the middle of the night to such disturbances. But eleven years later, as reported in the *Spectator* article entitled "Explain this one!" by reporter Mark McNeil, the secrets hidden in the walls of that Upper Wellington apartment were finally revealed.[2]

In the fall of 1982, Mike Cino's demolition firm was working at removing the building and adjacent hardware store in order for a parking lot to be developed there. During the demolition, one of his men mentioned he kept hearing strange sounds when he was pulling out the copper. But it wasn't until the walls were being brought down that the crew discovered something bizarre and shocking — the remains of a nineteenth-century tombstone were trapped inside a wall above the bedroom where Norm and Sherri Bilotti used to sleep.

The tombstone was apparently for a double grave. The top had an inscription that read OUR BABY and below that, on a pair of adjoined stones, were MARTH LOUISE, 1888 and EMMA GRACE, NON 9, 1879.

Cino couldn't explain what a tombstone might be doing in the walls or why somebody would have removed the tombstone from the neighbouring cemetery; but he did speculate that perhaps it had been used as some kind of support for the wall.

This intriguing discovery was a reminder of psychic Malcolm Bessent's strong belief that there was something hidden within the walls; of course, the connection between the dual tombstone and the hovering old woman with no legs could never be determined, but there is no denying that there does seem to be a connection there.

Was the ghost the Bilottis saw that of the woman who had been a previous tenant? Perhaps she was trying to draw somebody's attention to the desecration of her children's graves, as any bereaved living mother might do: the noises the construction workers heard during the demolition were just one last cry for help from this spirit.

Norm Bilotti returned to the demolition site and posed for a picture in the *Spectator*, holding the gravestone in front of the rubble of the building he used to live in. The look on his face when he saw the tombstone was not unlike the look of a man seeing a ghost. Except Bilotti didn't believe in ghosts.

"There has to be another explanation," he said.

CHAPTER NINETEEN

A WESTDALE GHOST

In the course of my research for this book, it was inevitable that people who found out what I was writing wanted to share their personal experiences. While I heard so very many interesting tales, there was one in particular that caught my interest. I think, perhaps, it is because of the approach I have taken with this book.

Yes, this is a book of ghost tales: true encounters with the supernatural. But I have done my best to look into the details in question, to seek out as many sources as possible, and to try to understand the "spooks" from a historical perspective. I make no claims of having any sort of unbiased approach, nor a supposed journalistic integrity in the way the tales have been written. But I did my best to stick close to the facts, and, where the facts were light, I believe I have tried to ensure that there was a balance in the presentation of the stories.

To that end, I share this story of a colleague I worked with at McMaster University. When he learned that I was working on a book of ghost stories for Dundurn, he offered to tell me a tale over coffee. Something happened to him several decades ago that still sends shivers down his spine.

When he told me the tale, I, too, experienced an eerie chill, and even as the story was unfolding, I knew it was something I wanted to include in this book.

This gentleman is an academic — a multi-disciplined, highly educated person who carefully thinks things through. He is a person I have never seen jumping to conclusions, and who approaches every task in a careful, methodical manner. He is not the type of person to get easily excited about something, nor to put much stock in things without carefully applying the scientific method — a handy fix-it sort of person who was known for carefully making things better; several people who worked with him on campus nicknamed him MacGyver. For that reason, I'll call him Angus, as this was the first name of the character made popular in that 1980s ABC television show.

At about the same time that Richard Dean Anderson was playing Angus MacGyver, my colleague Angus and his wife were living in an apartment in the older section of Hamilton. They found that the space wasn't large enough for them, so they got a house in Westdale. Their first couple of nights after moving in, there were some unusual sounds accompanied by the odd feeling that they were in kind of a strange place. "Usually when you move in to a new place you feel somewhat unsettled," Angus said. "But I had never felt uneasy like that before."

Angus and his wife, Linda, just shrugged that uneasy feeling off as "new move in" jitters. They reasoned that things hadn't been put away properly, most of their belongings were still in boxes, and it would take time to settle in and for the feeling to pass.

One afternoon, Angus was doing some work at home and thought he'd throw some clothes down the laundry chute; it was one of the older homes that had a chute from the top floor down to the basement. "That was when I heard these creaking noises down in the basement coming from up the laundry chute," he said. Angus described the noises as reminding him of the sound a person would make walking on the stairs.

Angus thought it was really unusual, since there was nobody else in the house, and immediately suspected that someone had gotten in and was snooping around. "My initial impression was that someone had been walking down the stairs, which was enough to make me uneasy because the doors were locked and there was supposedly nobody in the house." So he quietly went to the basement and things seemed very normal — nothing was out of place and there was nobody to be found.

In the manner that people rationalize things to themselves — particularly things that don't make sense or fit into the world as most people know it — Angus decided that it must have been something else he had heard, most likely noises that had carried in through the laundry chute from somewhere outside.

So he went back upstairs and resumed working. A little later, he heard a somewhat similar noise again, but more remote. This was likely because the laundry chute was closed. So he repeated his performance of walking downstairs cautiously. "And of course," Angus said, "there was nothing there the second time, either."

Two or three months passed, and Angus was working late one night on the main floor; he had been sitting in the living room with a notepad, sketching out some ideas for a project he was working on. Linda, who worked in Toronto and had a long commute ahead of her in the morning, had already gone to sleep. So when he heard the familiar creaking of footsteps coming from upstairs, he immediately jumped up to investigate. But again, he found nothing, and Linda was still sound asleep in her bed.

This repeated auditory phenomenon became a common occurrence. It continued like that for some time, almost to the point that Angus and his wife had gotten used to it.

But, just as Angus was settling into a routine that incorporated the noises, something more startling occurred. One night, he woke up and saw what he described as a hologram of a male standing in the doorway to his bedroom. Startled, Angus sat up, leaned forward, and tried to look closer to see what it was — he was convinced it was some sort of trick of the moon shining in and bouncing off a reflective surface of some sort.

But the instant he was up it disappeared.

Angus became determined that he was going to have to be more alert in the future so that when he woke up he didn't move, but merely opened his eyes to check things out first so as not to startle or disturb whatever might have been in his doorway.

It was about a week later that Angus woke up again in the middle of the night; this time for some inexplicable reason. There hadn't been any noise or other physical disturbance — he just woke up. This time Angus was disciplined enough not to toss the blanket aside and sit straight up, and when he looked out the doorway he saw the hologram again. It didn't seem all that three-dimensional, and it wasn't casting any sort of light, but he looked at it for a moment, just taking it in. That's when he very carefully slipped out from under the covers and got out of bed. The human figure standing in the doorway remained where it stood.

Upon closer inspection, he noticed that it was the size and shape of a man somewhere in the range of five and a half to six feet tall. There was no motion of arms, or any effort to make a motion or a step. The clothing the man wore wasn't distinct — he was non-descript and seemed relatively modern or contemporary. And though Angus couldn't see any lines on the man's face or any other distinguishing features, he had the impression that this was an elderly man. The figure wasn't hunched, but it wasn't standing erect like a soldier.

Angus got up and realized that he didn't have any feelings of anxiety. He regularly meditated, so knew the feeling of inner peace. And though he wasn't in quite the same relaxed state, he didn't have an uneasy feeling, certainly nothing like the previous experiences and the uneasy feelings he'd felt before, upon hearing strange noises in the house. He was simply at peace with what was there. There was no associated alarming feeling upon looking at what he describes as the hologram of this elderly gentleman.

He slowly stepped toward the figure standing in the doorway. It didn't disappear this time. He then deliberately opened his hand, because to him that was a kind of a sign of peace. "Then I slowly put my hand through the hologram," Angus said. "And it still didn't disappear. It wasn't until I pulled my hand back that it disappeared."

When his hand passed through the figure, he didn't feel anything: no chill, no warmth — it was as if his hand was passing through a beam of light. Angus noted that his hand had become more opaque as it passed through the body of the elderly man.

Angus and Linda talked to one of the neighbours not long after. The neighbour was a retired schoolteacher who was working around the garden and was curious about the fragrances coming out of the house due to cooking, so she offered them some herbs.

Out of the blue, the retired schoolteacher asked Angus an interesting question: "Have you heard any strange noises in your house?"

Angus said, "Why do you ask?"

"Oh," she said. "The people who had the house before you complained that they had heard very unusual noises in the house."

Angus asked what his predecessors attributed the noise to. She said she didn't know, but that prior to them, there had been some weird people living in the house for about a quarter of a century. That was the end of that conversation.

A few weeks after that, Angus was speaking with an older lady who lived on the other side of them. This woman needed some consolation because she'd had a disagreement with her eldest daughter. The woman was really broken-hearted, and she looked at Angus, held up her finger, and said, "When I die I'm going to come back and haunt that daughter of mine." Then she turned to Angus and commented that he should know something about that.

"What are you talking about?" Angus asked.

She said, "Because of the house you live in. You must have heard *something*."

Not long after, Angus and Linda decided that because they did a lot of travelling, they would move into a more condominium-type accommodation. Nothing else eerie had happened to them after his encounter with the spectre of the elderly man that one night, but Angus was always intrigued and wanted to find out more about the strange house in Westdale they had lived in.

One day, he went down to city hall to search the title on the house. They let him search the title all the way back to the building's construction, though he was still unable to determine the owners at that time. But the woman who was helping him held him in a piercing look, as if she knew something that she was keeping from Angus.

At one point, she asked why Angus would want to know this information. He made up a story and explained he was doing some research on the house. But the woman wouldn't give the name of the original owners of the house.

"Would you mind telling me why not?" Angus asked.

She said it was usually only architects and builders who needed to have that information — it was on a need-to-know basis.

So Angus never learned more about the house of strange noises and the ghostly elderly gentleman he had encountered standing in his bedroom doorway.

But what becomes even more curious isn't what Angus heard and saw in that house. The real question is what the city worker was keeping from Angus. What even more curious secrets were kept hidden on that house on Kenmore Street?

CHAPTER TWENTY

HAUNTED PUBS

Associate a place with drinking and late-night cavorting and you're likely to encounter more than a few unbelievable stories. Nonetheless, Hamilton has its share of haunted drinking establishments, and not just hauntings of barflies who are a constant fixture on a corner stool.

When one thinks about a pub, restaurant, or bar, one imagines a place continually filled with people from various walks of life, each carrying their own personal baggage, whether it's a lightly packed affair or something more foreboding and ominous. These are places where the extremes of emotions are felt, where heightened senses are played upon, and where drama can unfold quickly. The two musical extremes of wanting to party like its "1999" or drowning one's sorrows in another round of "One Bourbon, One Scotch, One Beer" often take place in this type of setting. So is it any wonder that such activity might have a ripple effect on the cosmic aura of a place?

This chapter takes a look at a few of the allegedly haunted pubs in the Hamilton area. I have just cleaned the bar in front of you; the seat is yours if you want it. Please join me as I pull back the tap and pour you a nice cold glass of speculative wonder.

A GHOST NAMED HARVEY

A bar called The Werx on Hughson Street in Hamilton has its share of regulars who are not all that different than Harvey. Unlike most, however, this one never leaves a tip, nor does he ever make a mess. You see, Harvey is a ghost.

Both customers and staff have seen or felt him; but they're okay with it. In fact, Harvey is a friendly and well-accepted resident ghost. The other patrons of the bar are tolerant of Harvey — perhaps because they know what it's like to be shunned for being different. You see, The Werx is a gay bar. Apart from a dining room, bar, and dance floor, it has a leather bar in the basement and holds leather and fetish parties once a month. The customers and staff are an outgoing, friendly, and accepting group — open-minded and happy to accept people for who and what they are.[1]

Harvey is, thus, just another visitor to their world, one who looks on from the great beyond and rarely ever causes any sort of fuss. He just shows up from time to time. Occasionally, he puts a scare into people, but mostly he just gets along and watches.

Harvey is regularly seen by customers and staff near the back of the bar and near the women's washrooms. Sometimes his presence is merely felt in terms of an inexplicable cold brush of something moving past. Other times he has even been seen looking in a window from the alley. Of course, the strange thing about that is, based upon the height of the window, Harvey would either have had to have been standing on a step-ladder or else floating three or four feet off of the alley floor.[2]

Most vote for the latter of the two.

Staff have had encounters with Harvey where he has actually tried to manipulate objects. Harvey has been known to start up and stop the vacuum cleaner as if playing with it and testing it out. He has also been known to turn lights back on after the bar manager completes the round of turning off all the lights at the end of a night. At times, after knowing for sure that he had turned all the lights off, manager Mike Panopolous has gone back, having forgotten something, to see that the lights were back on again.[3]

Panopolous has explained that Harvey is likely the ghost of a custodian who lived in an apartment in the building where The Werx is, but who died in a fire in the back. The building at 121 Hughson, which took on various different forms over the years, housed charities, fraternities, dancers, insurance agents, and photographers. It was even once a spice factory and served as a church. In 1980 it became a bar, and in 2002, The Werx opened.[4]

And it seems as if the tenants of The Werx have revived.

One tale involving Harvey has to do with a few employees casually chatting after the bar closed for the night. In the middle of their chatter, the piano in The Saffron Room started to play. They thought that was strange, since the door to that room had been locked and there was nobody else in the building. As they went to investigate, the piano music kept playing up until the point that they unlocked the door and opened it. When they threw open the door, the music abruptly stopped and they found nobody in the room.[5]

Not much is known about Harvey, the custodian who died as a result of the burns he received in the fateful fire. But you might just see or hear a story about Harvey if you were to head down to The Werx.[6]

Just don't expect him to join you out on the dance floor if your favourite song pops up in the DJ's mix.

WINKING GHOSTS

A pub located at 25 Augusta Street in Hamilton specializes in microbrewed beer. With at least twenty-two taps, it offers one of the broadest selections, from a standard core selection to a featured series of rotating brands and styles of beers. They have, over the years, served over 285 different beers produced by brewmasters from Ontario, Quebec, and Alberta, as well as selected European imports.

The atmosphere at Augusta's Winking Judge is devoted to good beer and offers a perfect place to hang out with old friends or to make new ones. But this pub also offers something that is not on their rather broad list of available brews: for more than ten years, they have also been home to a number of supernatural visitors. More than fifty sightings of the ghost of an elderly man have been reported by staff and patrons at the place often fondly referred to as "The Judge."[7]

The man, dressed in a dark suit and a top hat, strongly suggesting he is originally from a time long past, usually appears in the window of the men's washroom on the upper floor. He is sometimes seen from the other windows on the main floor, but more often than not haunts the men's washroom the way a barfly might haunt his favourite stool.[8]

There is nothing frightening or foreboding about his appearances. He is merely there one moment, a silent and eerie spectre, and then he disappears.[9]

Maria Italia, the bar owner, has explained that this elderly dark man, who is the most often seen ghost in the pub, isn't the only one. Some people have experienced what they thought was a cat brushing against their legs; amused that the bar had their own resident pet, something that usually gives a place some character, they would reach down to stroke the animal, only to find nothing there. Augusta's Winking Judge doesn't have a resident pet — at least not one that you need to feed and clean up after.[10]

Inexplicable wisps of smoke have been seen floating up the stairs even after Hamilton adopted a no smoking bylaw for bars and restaurants, and footsteps are sometimes heard, particularly when the bar is empty and there is nobody else in the building.[11]

Italia has even recounted memories of her daughter having interesting conversations by herself when she was about two years old. When questioned about whom she was speaking to, the little girl would simply answer that she was talking to the man.[12]

With too many nocturnal and eerie sightings and happenings at the bar, Maria and her husband, Bill Rea, welcomed a team of paranormal investigators to check things out. Covered in articles in the *Hamilton Spectator*, as well as via interviews with local radio personalities, the supernatural activities of this Augusta Street bar became well-known back in 2008.

The organization that the owners called in was called the Southern Ontario Paranormal Society (or SOPS), which was formed by Steve Genier in 2005. SOPS doesn't charge for its services, which involves investigating a site with more than $5,000 in equipment to attempt to document or record what it calls "hot spots" of ghostly activity.[13]

Having spent a long night in the bar with half a dozen investigators and three "sensitives" (psychics who are attuned to feel otherworldly activity and presences), Genier recorded something that hadn't been heard before, and it was picked up simultaneously by two independent recording devices in the basement. Slightly obscured by the hum of a nearby refrigerator, a child-like voice can be heard saying, "I can hear you."[14]

Hamilton resident Randy Hines wasn't surprised to learn that the pub was haunted. After reading about the SOPS investigation in the *Hamilton Spectator*, he contacted reporter Mark McNeil to add some history to the contemporary experiences.[15]

Before it was converted into a business establishment, the building used to be a home. Hines said that his grandparents used to live in the house from the mid 1930s until the mid 1970s and that, as a child, he always felt it was haunted. He reports having heard things such an footsteps walking upstairs and recalls being warned by his grandfather not to go up into the attic because the man, Gord, would get him.[16]

If Gord is indeed the name of the spectral man in the dark suit and top hat, the ghost regularly seen at Augusta's Winking Judge seems to have mellowed over time. While feeling uneasy and freaked out at seeing him, nobody has ever felt threatened by this otherworldly visitor.

Instead, he is just there, an intriguing and often celebrated ghost who doesn't appear to disrupt or to judge. A spirit content to mingle in a place where spirits of the natural world flow quite freely as well, he seems more inclined to linger and adds ambiance to the old Victorian building.

THE COACH AND LANTERN

The Coach and Lantern British Pub sits on a busy street in downtown Ancaster amid trendy boutique shops and beautiful sandstone buildings. There is a bustle in the air most afternoons, of both pedestrians and traffic. Most people who pass the third oldest building in Ancaster might marvel at the classic stone look and front fence with wrought-iron archway that leads through to the patio and entrance, but they are likely unaware of the bloody history of this site, nor of the ghosts that roam around to this day inside.

Originally built in the 1700s, the building at 384 Wilson Street burned down and was re-built in 1823. But between those times, the land bore witness to The Bloody Assize in Upper Canada, a series of trials held during the War of 1812. During the war, a number of settlers from the Niagara and London region had taken up arms against their neighbours. Several groups were taken prisoner, and in 1814, fifteen of the nineteen people charged were found guilty — eight of them were executed in an utterly barbaric fashion.[17]

Justice Thomas Scott's execution order on that site included a centuries-old British-style punishment for treason. On June

21, 1814, Scott pronounced the sentence for eight of the men: "You are to be drawn on hurdles to a place of execution, whence you are to be hanged by the neck, but not until you are dead, for you must be cut down while alive and your entrails taken out and burnt before your faces. Your heads then to be cut off and your bodies divided into four quarters to be at the King's disposal. May God have mercy on your souls."

The following month, the men were transported all the way down to a gallows that was located across the street from where Dundurn Castle now stands. So while they were not killed on that spot, it was near that very location where their fates were sealed.

In 1832 the building was re-built for George Rousseaux, and in the 1870s it became the Old Union Hotel. It was converted into apartments in the 1950s, and in 1980 it was converted yet again, this time into a restaurant.

The original owners of the restaurant had experienced a resident ghost, who they described as an old man in his sixties, slouched over as if he was working in a field. Believing him to be a farmer or caretaker who had died in one of the fires that destroyed the original building, the old man's stance, when seen, made complete sense to them. Wearing a plaid shirt and burlap pants, the ghost is said to have also worn a haggard expression on his face.

Those first owners of the pub, which was originally known as The Coach and Lantern English Pub (new ownership brought a slight modification to the name, substituting the word *English* with *British*), were allegedly frightened to stay in the building alone at any time of the day or night.

Bob Conway, the more recent owner, encountered a different ghost even before he purchased the restaurant he would reopen. When the bar was closed, Conway moved behind the counter in an effort to teach himself the art of pouring a beer from the tap. When he looked up from his task, he saw a man sitting in the bar, wearing a pair of old-fashioned green overalls. The man quickly vanished from sight.[18]

Conway reports that a waitress also saw a man lingering near the end of the bar one evening after the bar had closed. When she spotted him, he turned and headed down the hallway as if toward the washrooms. She followed him, but was shocked to note that he had simply vanished upon entering the hallway. He was nowhere to be found.[19]

Once, Conway said, a woman was feeding her grandson in a room upstairs. They were by themselves, enjoying a quiet moment of child and grandparent bonding, when the distinct voice of a man over her shoulder stated, "What a beautiful baby!" Startled, the woman turned to find that nobody was there.[20]

Local psychic and clairvoyant Michele Stableford reports having seen the same man that Conway did on one of his earliest visits to the pub. She had been sitting with a friend at one of the tables when she spotted a man in green coveralls walking across the room. The man turned, glanced at Stableford, and then continued walking across the room and through the wall. Stableford, who has become used to seeing extraordinary things her entire life, said she also received a distinct impression of the letter *J* upon seeing the ghost, believing his name might perhaps be John.[21]

Another time, a waitress spotted a man sitting at a table and turned to retrieve a menu to bring over to him. But when she looked back his way, the man had simply disappeared.

Bob Conway reported that more than one staff member has quit after an encounter with the supernatural in his pub: one cook was scared off by the constant approaching rush of footsteps in his direction. A dishwasher left after exclaiming that he simply could not take it anymore.

Conway, a friendly fellow with a cheerful attitude, doesn't come across as a man haunted by terrible things. He accepts the supernatural occurrences in a somewhat jovial manner and smiles when welcoming in the regular groups of ghost hunters he says like to come out on Friday nights to "have a little fun upstairs."

"Before I bought this place, I was very skeptical about ghosts and ghost stories," Conway said; then, with a shrug, he continued, "I'm a little less sceptical now."

The folks from Haunted Hamilton often suggest The Coach and Lantern as a good place to get great food and beer — and to enjoy the friendly staff and atmosphere of the 175-year-old building — before heading out on their historic ghost walk of the nearby Hermitage ruins.

The pub, which proudly boasts free Wi-Fi and fantastic live entertainment on its web page, makes just a small reference to the legends of ghosts and the fact that there's often something more in the air than the sounds of a great local band or the unseen signals of a wireless internet connection.

CONCLUSION

One of the great benefits of getting to work on a book like this is the amount of research I had to do. With virtually every single chapter, almost every tale, I felt the need to go back and look further into the history of a person or a place, and my research sessions likely ended up being more than twice of what they truly needed to be. Caught up in the magic of history coming alive on the pages of the book in front of me, or of the archived newspaper clippings I was poring over, I had to keep reminding myself to stop and make notes.

I find it ever so intriguing that while I was originally drawn by the tales born from the dark shadows, I regularly became pulled into the historic legacy of the city.

And, of course, just the other night, when I was taking a stroll along the mountain brow in my neighbourhood with my wife and my son, at three separate times, as we passed landmarks, such as a building that used to be part of Buchanan's Claremont estate, of the location of the Mountain View Hotel and of the Bruce Trail, I would pause to share a delightful and intriguing factoid I had learned that often hadn't even found its way into this book.

At one point during our walk, my wife Francine turned to me with a bemused smile on her face and said, "Writing this book has been really good for you."

"Indeed," I said, nodding my agreement.

And not just because of the interesting facts I had discovered and was now sharing with others, but because of the manner by which my appreciation for our neighbourhood and our city was continuing to grow.

To liberate a phrase Sir Isaac Newton was known for, if I have been able to appreciate and see great things about this city and its fascinating and rich history, it is because I have stood on the shoulders of giants: all of the men, women, and children who initially established Hamilton and over the countless decades have helped it grow into the fine city it is today.

A LOOK AT THE PEOPLE BEHIND HAUNTED HAMILTON GHOST WALKS - EVENTS

I knew that when I first began writing a book involving ghosts in the Hamilton area, I would be consulting with the folks from Haunted Hamilton Ghost Walks & Events. Founders Daniel Cumerlato and Stephanie Lechniak have been very generous with their time, resources, and the more than ten years of in-depth research they have conducted as part of their business.

The whole way through my journey of compiling information and collecting tales, they have shared personal accounts, detailed articles, suggestions for people I should talk to, and have welcomed me with open arms and friendly smiles. They have also been generous with their time, responding to my phone calls and emails as well as sitting down with me at length to be interviewed about what they do and some of the legends they have investigated.

For this reason, I thought it would be important to share a little bit of detail about their group and all that they offer to Hamilton, not just from an intriguing and paranormal viewpoint, but from a historical perspective.

Dan and Stephanie have been running Haunted Hamilton since 1999.

It all started when the couple, who were both born and raised in Hamilton, were living in Toronto. They had always been intrigued by supernatural events and, one evening were conducting an Ouija board session in their apartment with a microcassette recorder. They had had done the usual things one does when playing with an Ouija board and asked if there was a spirit presence. Eventually, the pointer on the board moved to YES and occasionally moved around providing non-descript responses to their question, but nothing much really happened.

It wasn't until they were done the session, which was held in an apartment lit only by the atmospheric light of candles, that they discovered something eerie had happened and which neither of them had noticed. When they were done and listened to the tape they could hear their voices in the background, somewhat muted and distant because the recorder was sitting a few feet away from them. But after they had said: "Spirit, are you there?" a very clear, breathy voice could be heard right up at the microphone, saying, *Yesss!*

"We slept with the lights on that night!" Daniel joked.

But that incident was the genesis of it all. Daniel and Stephanie went to a local Toronto paranormal group with their story but didn't hear anything back. So they posted about their experience on the Internet, and among the website hits they received, they heard from a couple of guys who were planning on doing a paranormal television show. Stephanie and Daniel met with them and the guys listened to the EVP. They were quite intrigued and spent a long time discussing the event the couple had experienced as well as sharing other stories. Nothing ever happened with them or the television show, but Daniel and Stephanie's interest in the paranormal had been piqued. During the discussion, the guys who were working on the television show had mentioned something they called "the murder house" in Hamilton.

Afterwards, Stephanie and Daniel learned they were speaking about the Bellevue Mansion in Hamilton and they spent a great deal of time doing research on this building, discovering the tales surrounding it were akin to the legends associated with *The Amityville Horror*.

The two visited the mansion during the day. "Mostly because we were too frightened to visit the home in the middle of the night," Stephanie joked. Stephanie also went to her parents' home in Hamilton, snuck into her father's closet, and "borrowed" her father's rather expensive 35mm camera.

They entered the Bellevue Mansion, which was wide open, and marvelled at the sights, such as pieces of the stairwell missing and a tree growing up through the dumbwaiter area, and spent about an hour taking notes about and pictures of this historic building. Their visit wouldn't be complete, however, without checking out the Widow's Walk, where they saw the most beautiful view of the city.

They felt a connection to the house the second they stepped into it. The controversy about the house interested them so much that they started a website called Disappearing History as well as a site dedicated to ghosts and the supernatural. They wanted the stories of the disappearing history of the Hamilton area and these beautiful landmarks to be heard.

The ghostly tales, however, are what drew most visitors to their website, so they evolved the historically focused articles to include a supernatural flavour. Haunted Hamilton isn't there for the shock factor but instead to document and report. Yes, there is entertainment in the telling of their ghost stories, but never at the expense of the history.

"There's a respect that is given to the story," Daniel said. Respect for the person's legitimate story is what Stephanie, Daniel, and their team are all about. And while they prefer the term *Paranormal Investigators* to ones such as *Ghostbusters*, they're flexible in how people refer to them.

"We used the hate the term *Ghost Hunters,*" Daniel said. "But you've got to have a sense of humour and learn to go with the flow." Both Stephanie and Daniel have taught themselves to roll with the terms that become popular for people describing their theatrical approach to sharing Hamilton's spooky history.

In 2003, the same year that they started the ghost walks, a tour of various haunted locations in Hamilton's downtown core, they won two Tourism Hamilton awards: one for the best rookie of the year and another for the best new tourism idea. At a time when attracting people to the downtown core of Hamilton was a critical venture for the city, Haunted Hamilton managed to host huge groups of walking tours that celebrated Hamilton's historic buildings and people. It was ironic that their walks and tales of scary things going bump in the night were leading toward people feeling less scared to be downtown.

The night they received those two awards was the moment they first realized that this was something more than a hobby — this was something they could do full time.

They have since created multiple different ghost walks, as well as non-supernatural walks designed to entice people with details of Hamilton's rich history. Their Hamilton's Dark Past tour appeals more to the history and true crime buffs than to those interested in ghosts. The Victorian Parlour Ghost Stories evening they host in the old Scottish Rite building in Hamilton is a throwback to the classic verbally shared tales from yesteryear. It is ideal for those who wondered what it might be like to enjoy the unique magic of verbal storytelling, either from the age of Charles Dickens, or, as more recently, when Canada's own Robertson Davies spent eighteen consecutive years sharing oral ghost stories as part of annual Christmas celebrations at Massey College in Toronto.

In April 2011 they opened a museum of the paranormal (*www.MuseumOfTheParanormal.ca*) in Niagara-on-the-Lake at 118A Queen Street. The museum is Canada's only space dedicated to everything dark, creepy, and paranormal. In it they carry a range of products, from the fun, spooky novelty items you might expect, to beautiful gemstones, candles, and paranormal tools. But the museum is also home to one of the world's largest personal collections of post-mortem photography (yes, that would be photos of the dead), as well as displays of the world's most famous ghost photos, haunted dolls, and modern haunted locations in North America. Ultimately, the shop is dedicated to paranormal history, and that makes it rather unique.

The group conducts regular out-of-town bus tours as well as an annual costume ball for Halloween and continues to combine their interest in the paranormal and their respect for the city they so love and cherish. "People don't even know the rich history we have in Hamilton," Stephanie said. But, thanks to the efforts of Stephanie, Daniel, and their team, more people walk away with a better understanding of their city and the people who made it what it is today.

STEPHANIE AND DANIEL'S TEAM OF GHOST GUIDES

Ghost Guide George

George Sanford is an actor, composer, choreographer, poet, and playwright. He has been a performer for more than forty years and has been on stage, radio, TV, and video. He has a wealth of stage experience and theatre knowledge. He was one of the creators of the Sheridan College musical theatre program and has taught theatre arts at all levels of education. His business background is extensive, and he has found a unique and exciting way to combine his love and skill in the arts with the changing landscape of business and industry, in both the private and public sectors.

Established in 1999, Haunted Hamilton is one of the oldest paranormal groups still in existence in all of North America.

Lady Elizabeth

Lady Elizabeth, also known as Sue Hilton, has been involved in theatre for most of her life — after performing in *A Christmas Carol* with Simcoe Little Theatre while in public school, she was "bitten." Over two decades, she performed with Simcoe Little Theatre, Lighthouse Festival Theatre, and the Academy Theatre in Lindsay, Ontario. She attained her B.F.A. in acting from the University of Windsor and performed in numerous productions, such as Sam Shepherd's *A Lie of the Mind*, Michel Tremblay's *The Real World?*, *Guys and Dolls*, *Waiting for the Parade*, and many others. She has done children's theatre, tours, studio workshops, improv comedy, and a little bit of television (and is convinced her part is on a cutting room floor somewhere). After a lengthy hiatus to raise her son, she is thrilled to be back in front of the crowds doing what she loves most — entertaining!

Jack Lawrence

Jack, also known as Derk Ewert, has been intensely involved in the performing arts since a very young age. He devoted his entire high school experience to performing on stage and in the Sears Drama Festival and has put on fifteen major productions. He has been awarded four awards for acting through the Sears Festival while attending the St. Catharines Collegiate Institute and has also put on shows with the St. Thomas Players and the Carousel Players. An enthusiastic actor and musician, he is currently attending Brock University, working on his Honours Bachelor of Arts in Dramatic Arts degree. Being somewhat sensitive to the paranormal, he has always been interested in his experiences and hearing the experiences of others. He hopes you enjoy his playing on our haunted piano at the Museum of the Paranormal if you attend his tours and he diabolically asks, with a rue grin, if you would like to hear a story.

Daniel "Rook" Holbrooke

"Rook" (Daniel Wooster) is a trained actor who has played a wide array of roles in film, television, and theatre productions. Performance has been his life since before he can even remember, and he relies on the character of his loving and supportive parents not to divulge embarrassing stories of his exploits. Rook received his education from both Humber College and the University of Toronto in marketing and public relations. Combined with his passion for both performing and the paranormal, Rook was a welcome addition to Haunted Hamilton's team.

Lady Rowenna

Lady Rowenna is well known for her love of the arts. In her human form, known as Lauren, she is a dedicated actress, dancer, and singer. Her love for the arts began as a little girl when she played elaborate dress-up games with her sister, and it grew larger as she earned the part of the evil queen in her school musical, *Once Upon a Mattress*, in her grade twelve year. Lauren also loves writing short stories, but her biggest love is for visual art. Lauren begins her first year of visual arts studies at Brock University in the fall. Above all, her love for the supernatural and paranormal is undying.

Lady Lilith

Born and raised as Libby MacEachern, Lady Lilith has been acting dramatically on and off stage since she was young. An avid actress and singer, Lady Lilith has been in productions at the Firehall Theatre in Niagara Falls and Lakeshore Catholic High School in Port Colborne. Currently she is studying theatre at York University in Toronto and hopes to enter into the production field. Lady Lilith is all fun and games until she calls upon her Dark Passengers to aid her in retelling the stories of their restless spirits. Her keen interests in the paranormal make Lady Lilith a beautiful and deadly addition to the Haunted Hamilton team.

Lady Catharine

Lady Catharine (Cathy Ormerod) has been involved in the arts since she was a small child. Whether it was singing, acting, or visual, she has always found joy in the arts. She recently graduated with a degree in theatre from Brock University. In the last year, Cathy has switched her study focus from theatre to travel, which has also been a passion for several years. She has toured Europe, the Southern Caribbean, Eastern Canada, and lived in Florida for a summer while participating in the International College Program at Walt Disney World. She is excited to continue her adventures around the world as an international tour manager, focusing on

Europe and the rich history within. Lady Catharine welcomes you to her hometown of Niagara-on-the-Lake, to stroll through town and discover the haunted history within the jewel of Niagara.

Lady Bethany

Bethany, or as she's known in this century, Stef, has been performing in some form or another for as long as she can remember. It all started with putting on plays for her family as a child and eventually led her to studying theatre full-time at the University of Toronto. She has acted for stage, in short films, and worked in Toronto as a background actor. Stef's favourite acting experience was playing a Victorian vampire character that she had developed over several years, at Canada's Wonderland's Halloween Haunt. Along with her husband, Wayne, they became the two most well-known characters from that event over the four years they worked there. As for the spooky stuff, Stef has always had an interest in the paranormal, as she has been feeling strange things since she was a child. A self-proclaimed empath, she and her husband have travelled all over North America visiting haunted places to not only see what they may feel, but also because of their love for historic buildings. Stef currently lives in a Victorian manor house built in 1872 and shares her home with some permanent supernatural residents.

Lady Renée

Thirty years ago, Renée Baillargeon began her career as a professional actor, choreographer, and playwright and now works primarily as a director, adjudicator, and performer. She has performed and directed across Canada, from the Victoria Symphony in British Columbia to the Grenfel Players of Newfoundland. An adjunct professor of physical theatre at Niagara University, New York, she has also taught and directed at Brock, Memorial, Université de Moncton, and the University of Windsor. Renée, a bilingual graduate of the physical theatre school "Jacques LeCoq" in Paris and the University of Windsor B.F.A. program, also received her M.A. from the University of Paris III for her research on the contemporary American Musical.

Lady Jade

Terri Jade Pentlichuk is an artist of all kinds. Professionally, she's a graphic designer, but she is also an avid musician/singer/ songwriter/actor. She's studied many different art genres over the years and has performed on and off the stage for both music and drama. Currently she is a board member of the Dunnville Community Theatre. It is with great pleasure that Terri walks with Haunted Hamilton, for she has always had a deep interest in not only the supernatural but also the history that is involved in the stories. So much so that she visits historical locations as often as she can in her spare time. Known to some as "Cemeterri" for her insatiable love of all things dark and unusual, perhaps she will tickle your "scary bone" with her tales of the macabre.

Ghost Guide James

James Pettitt is an actor, musician, and writer. He has appeared both on and off stage and screen since he was five years old, appearing in over twenty plays, musicals, and movies combined. His awards include Best Actor at the International Teen Movie Festival 2002. James now teaches theatre arts to young children at Theatre Aquarius. He is an avid ghost and history enthusiast and is no newcomer to ghost hunting and things of that nature, as he has been active in the field for the last six years and has an abundance of personal ghost stories, which he is more than happy to share. James is thrilled to have been a part of the

Haunted Hamilton ghost walks since the very beginning and hopes to scare the living daylights out of you soon!

Lady Claire

Claire Rouleau is a singer/actor who recently completed a degree in child and youth studies at Brock University. Claire has been involved in the performing arts ever since she can remember and little brings her greater joy. She is thrilled to finally be pursuing studies in theatre full-time this fall. Recent roles include Nadia in the Canadian premiere of *bare* (Waters Edge Productions), the Beggar Woman in *Sweeney Todd* (Garden City Productions), Ariel in *Footloose* (Brock Musical Theatre), Alice Waters in *Twilight Los Angeles, 1992* (Brock Connections), and Lucy in *Dog Sees God* (This is N.A.M). Claire also directed and performed in *The Vagina Monologues* this year through the Feminist Action Collective of St. Catharines and has had the privilege to perform the national anthems at Toronto Raptors and Ottawa Senators games. Lady Claire delights in her moonlight strolls around the so seemingly peaceful Niagara-on-the-Lake, but invites you to join her and learn of its true history and subsequent horrors.

Lady Juliet Ravensdale

Lady Juliet was born on October 31, 1900, in the small town of Sour Spring, Ontario, which might explain her sour and crass personality (she can unexpectedly use her twisted humour against you). She now dwells in the quaint cemetery tucked behind Ruthven Park in Cayuga, Ontario. She said, "This is the one place that feels like home — where I can finally feel alone." Recently, she can be spotted on ghost walks such as Haunted Hamilton's Custom House and is known to hide in the ruins during the famous Hermitage walks.

Sometimes, she is summoned by Dan and Stephanie on the *Haunted Hamilton Radio Show,* where she often tells disturbing and scary stories that few people dare to tell. She is ashamed to admit that in her recent learning to drive, her car is still parked on the roof of McMaster (or local) University.

The Dead Dude

This mysterious cloaked figure has been spotted on several of Haunted Hamilton's ghost walks. Sometimes you won't even know he's there, while at other times, he'll be there to gently direct the light your way. They say he's dead, but he never stays around long enough for us to find out!

The Dark Widow

You'll never know when she'll appear, but the Dark Widow of Haunted Hamilton makes her way from place to place in everlasting mourning. She'll never say a word, she'll never speak again. But maybe, just maybe, you'll become acquainted with her on the next ghost walk!

You can read more about Daniel, Stephanie, their team, and the various things they offer to the historical and paranormal communities of the Hamilton region by visiting their websites at *www.hauntedhamilton.com* and *www.ghostwalks.com*.

NOTES

Chapter One: The Custom House

1. Alexander Hamilton Wingfield, "The Woman in Black," in *Poems and Songs: In Scotch and English* (Hamilton: The "Times" Book and Job Office, 1873), 252.
2. Worker's Arts and Heritage Centre, "A Brief History of the Custom House in Hamilton," *www.wahc-museum.ca/a-house.php*.
3. *Ibid.*
4. *Ibid.*
5. *Ibid.*
6. *Ibid.*
7. *Ibid.*
8. Haunted Hamilton, "The Custom House," *www.hauntedhamilton.com/local_customshouse.html*.
9. Worker's Arts and Heritage Centre, "A Brief History."
10. *Ibid.*
11. *Ibid.*
12. Peter Klaassen, "Local Haunts: The Custom House," *View* (2005): 18.

13. *Ibid.*
14. Wingfield, "The Woman in Black," 252–53.
15. "Robert Peel," *http://en.wikipedia.org/wiki/Robert_Peel.*

Chapter Two: The Ghosts of Dundurn Castle

1. Edward Smith, *Dundurn Castle: Sir Allan MacNab and His Hamilton Home* (Toronto: James Lorimer & Company, 2007), 55.
2. Bailey Melville, *The History of Dundurn Castle and Sir Allan MacNab,* (Toronto: W.L. Griffin, 1943), 18.
3. City of Hamilton, "Dundurn Castle," *www.hamilton.ca/NR/exeres/07027F55-5B50-4553-807E-610C99B16EF6,frameless.htm?NRMODE=Published.*
4. *Ibid.*
5. Smith, *Dundurn Castle,* 5.
6. Smith, *Dundurn Castle,* 6.
7. *Ibid.,* 10.
8. City of Hamilton, "Dundurn Castle."
9. *Ibid.*
10. Haunted Hamilton, "Dundurn Castle," *www.hauntedhamilton.com/local_dundurn.html.*
11. Paul Wilson, "Did Ghostly Guest Crash Wedding?" *Hamilton Spectator,* August 17, 2000.
12. History to the People, "Canadian Castles Part IV: Dundurn Castle," *http://historytothepeople.ca/2010/10/canadian-castles-part-iv-dundurn-castle-hamilton-ontario.*
13. "Dundurn Castle," *http://en.wikipedia.org/wiki/Dundurn_Castle.*
14. History to the People, "Canadian Castles Part IV."
15. "Dundurn Castle," *http://en.wikipedia.org/wiki/Dundurn_Castle.*
16. John Robert Columbo, *Mysteries of Ontario* (Toronto: Hounslow Press, 1999), 106.
17. Smith, *Dundurn Castle,* 45.

Chapter Three: Bellevue Mansion

1. Daniel Cumerlato, "Beauty's Gone: The Story of Bellevue," *www. hauntedhamilton.com/disappearinghistory/dh_1_bellevue.html*.
2. Nancy DeHart and Carmelina Prete, "Faces & Places," *The Hamilton Spectator*, December 2, 1997.
3. Cumerlato, "Beauty's Gone."
4. David Cumming, *Hamilton's Heritage Volume 5: Reasons for Designation Under Part IV of the Ontario Heritage Act* (Hamilton: City of Hamilton Planning and Development Department, 2004), 83.
5. *Ibid.*
6. Cumerlato, "Beauty's Gone."
7. *Ibid.*
8. Rick Hughes, "Landmark Bellevue Mansion Headed for Demolition," *Hamilton Spectator*, August 23, 2000.
9. Haunted Hamilton, "The Historic Bellevue House," *www. hauntedhamilton.com/local_bellevue_pics.html*.
10. *Ibid.*
11. Paul Wilson, "Bellevue Was a Victim of the Times and the Man" *Hamilton Spectator*, September 5, 2002.
12. Nancy DeHart, "Bellevue: To Preserve or Destroy," *Hamilton Spectator*, December 30, 1997.

Chapter Four: Battlefield House Museum

1. Battlefield House Museum, "The War of 1812 — Niagara to Stoney Creek," *www.battlefieldhouse.ca/war1812.asp*.
2. *Ibid.*
3. Canada's Historic Places, "Battlefield Monument — Stoney Creek Battlefield Park," *www.historicplaces.ca/en/rep-reg/place-lieu.aspx?id=8165*.
4. Battlefield House Museum, "Battlefield Monument," *www. battlefieldhouse.ca/monument.asp*.

5. *Ibid.*
6. *Ibid.*
7. *Ibid.*
8. Battlefield House Museum, "Battlefield House," *www. battlefieldhouse.ca/house.asp.*
9. Alma Dick-Lauder, *Pen and Pencil Sketches of Wentworth Landmarks* (Hamilton: Spectator Printing Company, Ltd., 1897), 130–31.
10. Haunted Hamilton, "Stoney Creek's Battlefield House Museum," *www.hauntedhamilton.com/local_battlefield.html.*
11. Battlefield House Museum, "Battlefield House."
12. *Ibid.*
13. *Ibid.*
14. *Ibid.*
15. *Ibid.*
16. Battlefield House Museum, "The Re-enactment of the Battle of Stoney Creek," *www.battlefieldhouse.ca/reenactment.asp.*
17. Haunted Hamilton, "Stoney Creek's Battlefield House Museum."
18. *Ibid.*
19. *Ibid.*

Chapter Five: The Devil's Punchbowl

1. Hamilton Conservation Authority, "Passive Areas," *www. conservationhamilton.ca/passive-areas.*
2. *Ibid.*
3. Ontario Trails Council, "Dofasco 2000 Trail," *www. ontariotrails.on.ca/trails-a-z/dofasco-2000-trail.*
4. City of Waterfalls, "Devil's Punchbowl," *www.cityofwaterfalls. ca/devil_punchbowl.html.*
5. Hamilton Conservation Authority, "Passive Areas."
6. Haunted Hamilton, "Devil's Punch Bowl," *www.haunted hamilton.com/local_punchbowl.html.*

7. *Ibid.*

8. *Ibid.*

9. *Ibid.*

10. *Ibid.*

11. City of Waterfalls, "Devil's Punchbowl."

12. Wikipedia, "Super Dave Osborne," *http://en.wikipedia.org/wiki/Super_Dave_Osborne.*

13. Wikipedia, "Devil's Punch Bowl (Hamilton, Ontario)," *http://en.wikipedia.org/wiki/Devil%27s_Punch_Bowl_%28Hamilton,_Ontario%29.*

Chapter Six: The Hermitage

1. Wikipedia, "The Hermitage (Hamilton, Ontario)," *http://en.wikipedia.org/wiki/The_Hermitage_%28Hamilton,_Ontario%29.*

2. Haunted Hamilton, "Ghost Walk of the Hermitage Ruins," *www.hauntedhamilton.com/ghostwalks/hermitage.htm.*

3. Haunted Hamilton, "The Hermitage," *www.hauntedhamilton.com/local_hermitage.html.*

4. Margaret Houghton, *The Hamiltonians: 100 Fascinating Lives* (Toronto: James Lorimer & Company Ltd, 2003), 84.

5. Haunted Hamilton, "The Hermitage."

6. Rob Howard, "The Second Ghost," *The Hamilton Spectator,* October 31, 2000.

7. Haunted Hamilton, "The Hermitage."

8. Ancaster History, "Architectural Styles of Stone Buildings of Ancaster," *www.ancasterhistory.ca/ancaster-stone-buildings.php.*

9. Houghton, *The Hamiltonians,* 53.

10. *Ibid.*

11. Alma Dick-Lauder, *Pen and Pencil Sketches of Wentworth Landmarks* (Hamilton: Spectator Printing Company, Ltd., 1897), 18.

12. *Ibid.,* 123.

13. *Ibid.*, 18.

Chapter Seven: Auchmar House

1. Wikipedia, "Carpenter Gothic," *http://en.wikipedia.org/wiki/Carpenter_Gothic.*
2. Haunted Hamilton, "Auchmar: Prominence and History on the Mountain," *www.hauntedhamilton.com/disappearinghistory/dh_8_auchmar.html.*
3. Wikipedia, "Isaac Buchanan," *http://en.wikipedia.org/wiki/Isaac_Buchanan.*
4. *Ibid.*
5. Auchmar, "About the Honourable Isaac Buchanan," *www.auchmar.info/about_buchanan.html.*
6. Wikipedia, "Isaac Buchanan."
7. Auchmar, "About Auchmar," *www.auchmar.info/about_auchmar.html.*
8. *Ibid.*
9. Haunted Hamilton, "Auchmar."
10. Auchmar, "About Auchmar."
11. *Ibid.*
12. *Ibid.*
13. *Ibid.*
14. Alma Dick-Lauder, *Pen and Pencil Sketches of Wentworth Landmarks* (Hamilton: Spectator Printing Company, Ltd, 1897), 55.
15. *Ibid.*, 54.
16. Auchmar, "About Auchmar."
17. Haunted Hamilton, "Auchmar."
18. *Ibid.*
19. Haunted Hamilton, "The Ghosts of Auchmar Estate," *www.hauntedhamilton.com/local_auchmar.html.*
20. *Ibid.*
21. *Ibid.*

22. *Ibid.*

23. Jeff Mahoney, "A Quick Visit to Black Hole High," *Hamilton Spectator*, September 25, 2002.

24. Haunted Hamilton, "Ghosts on the Set of Black Hole High," *www.ghostwalks.com/local_auchmar_blackholehigh.html.*

25. Haunted Hamilton, "Ghosts of Auchmar Estate."

Chapter Eight: Woodend

1. Haunted Hamilton, "Woodend: The Haunting of John Heslop," *www.hauntedhamilton.com/local_woodend.html.*

2. Margaret Houghton, *The Hamiltonians: 100 Fascinating Lives* (Toronto: James Lorimer & Company Ltd, 2003), 79.

3. Edward Butts, *Murder: Twelve True Stories of Homicide in Canada* (Toronto, Dundurn Press, 2011), 71.

4. *Ibid.*

5. Haunted Hamilton, "Woodend."

6. Butts, *Murder*, 71.

7. Haunted Hamilton, "Woodend."

8. Butts, *Murder*, 72.

9. *Ibid.*

10. *Ibid.*

11. *Ibid.*, 73–81.

12. Houghton, *Hamiltonians*, 80.

13. Butts, *Murder*, 81.

14. Wikipedia, "Hamilton Conservation Authority," *http://en.wikipedia.org/wiki/Hamilton_Conservation_Authority.*

15. Haunted Hamilton, "Woodend."

Chapter Nine: Burkholder Cemetery

1. Barber Family Genealogical Site, "Jacob Burkholder," *www.laurence barber.ca/Families/People/Barber/Roberts/Nicholson/Burkholder/jacob_burkholder.htm.*

2. Haunted Hamilton, "Burkholder United Church and Cemetery," *www.laurencebarber.ca/Families/People/Barber/Roberts/Nicholson/Burkholder/jacob_burkholder.htm*.

3. Margaret Houghton, *The Hamiltonians: 100 Fascinating Lives* (Toronto: James Lorimer & Company Ltd, 2003), 31.

4. *Ibid.*, 32.

5. *Ibid.*

6. Haunted Hamilton, "Burkholder United Church and Cemetery."

7. *Ibid.*

8. *Ibid.*

Chapter Ten: Whitehern Mansion

1. Whitehern Museum Archives, "Tower Poetry Society Contest at Whitehern — Winning Sonnets — 2005," *www.whitehern.ca/result.php?doc_id=Box%2014-112*.

2. Doug Foley, "The McQuesten Legacy," *The Hamilton Spectator*, July 19, 2008.

3. Historical Hamilton, "Whitehern," *http://historicalhamilton.com/special-features/favourite-locations/whitehern*.

4. Wikipedia, "Whitehern," *http://en.wikipedia.org/wiki/Whitehern*.

5. City of Hamilton, "Whitehern Historic House and Garden," *www.hamilton.ca/CultureandRecreation/Arts_Culture_And_Museums/HamiltonCivicMuseums/Whitehern*.

6. Dictionary of Canadian Bibliography Online, "McQuesten, Calvin," *www.biographi.ca/EN/009004-119.01-e.php?id_nbr=5704*.

7. Whitehern Museum Archives, "Family: Isaac Baldwin McQuesten of Whitehern," *http://www.whitehern.ca/c_isaac.php*.

8. Margaret Houghton, *The Hamiltonians: 100 Fascinating Lives* (Toronto: James Lorimer & Company Ltd, 2003), 111–13.

9. Wikipedia, "Thomas McQuesten," *http://en.wikipedia.org/wiki/Thomas_McQuesten*.

10. Haunted Hamilton, "Whitehern," *www.hauntedhamilton. com/local_whitehern.html.*

11. *Ibid.*

12. Haunted Hamilton, "Whitehern."

13. Mary J. Anderson, *The Life Writings of Mary Baker McQuesten: Victorian Matriarch* (Waterloo: Wilfrid Laurier University Press, 2004), 52.

Chapter Eleven: Mount Albion Falls

1. Alma Dick-Lauder, *Pen and Pencil Sketches of Wentworth Landmarks* (Hamilton: Spectator Printing Company, Ltd, 1897), 133.

2. Wikipedia, "Albion Falls," *http://en.wikipedia.org/wiki/ Albion_Falls.*

3. Haunted Hamilton, "Lover's Leap at Albion Falls," *www. hauntedhamilton.com/local_albionfalls.html.*

4. Wikipedia, "Mount Albion, Ontario," *http://en.wikipedia. org/wiki/Mount_Albion,_Ontario.*

5. City of Waterfalls, "Albion Falls," *http://www.cityofwaterfalls. ca/albionfalls.html.*

6. *Ibid.*

7. Dick-Lauder, *Pen and Pencil Sketches*, 134.

8. *Ibid.*, 134–35.

9. Wikipedia, "Rocco Perri," *http://en.wikipedia.org/wiki/ Rocco_Perri.*

10. Taxi Library, "Canadian Taxi Driver Homicides, 1917–2007: Fred Genessee," *www.taxi-library.org/canada/1-g12.htm.*

11. Wikipedia, "Evelyn Dick," *http://en.wikipedia.org/wiki/ Evelyn_Dick.*

12. Marcy and Giasone Italiano, "Over the Hill," *www.slimeguy. com/gruesomeCDOvertheHill.htm.*

13. Bill Freeman, *Hamilton: A People's History* (Toronto: James Lorimer & Company Ltd., 2001), 151.

14. Mark McNeil, "1946: The Year a City Lost Its Innocence," *Hamilton Spectator*, February 28, 2006.
15. Brian Vallée, *The Torso Murder: The Untold Story of Evelyn Dick* (Toronto: Key Porter Books, 2001), 104.
16. *Ibid.*, 98–99.
17. Gwyn (Jocko) Thomas, "Remembering the Notorious Mrs. Dick," *Toronto Star*, March 17, 2002.
18. "Sensational Evidence in Murder Case," *Ottawa Citizen*, October 15, 1946: 14.
19. Vallée, *Torso Murder*, 160.

Chapter Twelve: Dundas District Elementary School

1. Wikipedia, "Dundas District Public School," *http:// en.wikipedia.org/wiki/Dundas_District_Public_School*.
2. *Ibid.*
3. *Ibid.*
4. *Ibid.*
5. *Ibid.*
6. *Ibid.*
7. Stan Nowak, "Christmas Turns Tragic for Holiday Special," *Ancaster News*, November 5, 2000.
8. *Ibid.*
9. Erin Rankin, "Hair-Raising Local Legends Live On," *Ancaster News*, Oct 29, 2004.
10. *Ibid.*
11. A.S. Mott, *Haunted Schools* (Edmonton: Ghost House Books, 2003), 162.
12. Suzanne Bourrett, "Haunted by a Pact," *Hamilton Spectator*, October 26, 1996.
13. *Ibid.*
14. Haunted Hamilton, "Dundas District Elementary School," *www.hauntedhamilton.com/9_hhnews.html*.
15. Haunted Hamilton, "Submissions: Dundas District," *www.*

hauntedhamilton.com/submissions_read_56.html.

16. Craig Campbell, "Innovation Group Looks at District Uses," *Dundas Star News*, March 9, 2007.

17. Jeremy Grimaldi, "Old Dundas School Being Transformed," *Hamilton Spectator*, August 4, 2010.

18. Craig Campbell, "Investigations Closed in Photographer's Fall," *Dundas Star News*, June 22, 2011.

Chapter Thirteen: The Hamilton Armouries

1. Wikipedia, "The Royal Hamilton Light Infantry (Wentworth Regiment)," http://en.wikipedia.org/wiki/The_Royal_Hamilton _Light_Infantry_%28Wentworth_Regiment%29.

2. *Ibid.*

3. Haunted Hamilton, "The Hamilton Armouries," *www. hauntedhamilton.com/local_armouries.html.*

4. Collections Canada, "Canadian Forces Before 1914," *www. collectionscanada.gc.ca/genealogy/022-909.005-e.html.*

5. Haunted Hamilton, "Hamilton Armouries."

6. *Ibid.*

7. Wikipedia, "John Weir Foote," *http://en.wikipedia.org/wiki/ John_Weir_Foote.*

8. *Ibid.*

9. Haunted Hamilton, "Hamilton Armouries."

10. *Ibid.*

Chapter Fourteen: The Waterdown Ghost

1. Wikipedia, "Great Depression in Canada," *http://en. wikipedia.org/wiki/Great_Depression_in_Canada.*

2. Haunted Hamilton, "The Waterdown Ghost," *www.haunted hamilton.com/17_waterdown_waterdownghost.html.*

3. Wikipedia, "Waterdown, Ontario," *http://en.wikipedia.org/ wiki/Waterdown,_Ontario.*

4. Haunted Hamilton, "Waterdown Ghost."
5. *Ibid.*
6. *Ibid.*
7. *Ibid.*
8. *Ibid.*
9. *Ibid.*
10. *Ibid.*
11. Wikipedia, "Waterdown, Ontario."

Chapter Fifteen: Haunted McMaster

1. Wikipedia, "McMaster University," *http://en.wikipedia.org/wiki/McMaster_University.*
2. *Ibid.*
3. Haunted Hamilton, "The Keg Mansion," *www.hauntedhamilton.com/57_article_kegmansion.html.*
4. Wikipedia, "Keg Mansion," *http://en.wikipedia.org/wiki/Keg_Mansion.*
5. Haunted Hamilton, "Keg Mansion."
6. *Ibid.*
7. *Ibid.*
8. Simica Kabir, "There's a Man Living at Wallingford," *Silhouette*, September 21, 2000.

Chapter Sixteen: The Tivoli Theatre

1. Haunted Hamilton, "The Tivoli Theatre," *www.hauntedhamilton.com/62_article_tivolitheatre_1.html.*
2. Haunted Hamilton, "The Disappearance of Ambrose Small," *www.hauntedhamilton.com/gotw_ambrosesmall.html.*
3. Wikipedia, "Ambrose Small," *http://en.wikipedia.org/wiki/Ambrose_Small.*
4. Haunted Hamilton, "Disappearance of Ambrose Small."
5. *Ibid.*

6. Haunted Hamilton, "Tivoli Theatre."
7. Haunted Hamilton, "The Ghosts of the Tivoli Theatre," *www. hauntedhamilton.com/62_article_tivolitheatre_3.html.*

Chapter Seventeen: Gus's Ghost Story

1. "His Weird Experience with Tricky Spooks. The House Is Said to Be Haunted," *Hamilton Herald*, August 16, 1902.

Chapter Eighteen: The Tombstone Ghost

1. John Bryden: "In Search of a Ghost," *Hamilton Spectator*, November 27, 1971.
2. Mark McNeil, "Explain This One! Tombstone Found in Home 11 Years after Spirit Seen," *Hamilton Spectator*, October 26, 1982.

Chapter Twenty: Haunted Pubs

1. John Burman, "'Harvey' the Tolerant, Friendly Ghost; He's a Regular at Downtown Bar," *Hamilton Spectator*, October 27, 2005.
2. *Ibid.*
3. *Ibid.*
4. *Ibid.*
5. *Ibid.*
6. *Ibid.*
7. Mark McNeil, "Ghostly Spirits; Pub owner Welcomes Paranormal Sleuths to Find the Unbottled Spirits that Are Haunting Her Downtown Building," *Hamilton Spectator*, February 14, 2008.
8. *Ibid.*

9. *Ibid.*
10. *Ibid.*
11. *Ibid.*
12. *Ibid.*
13. *Ibid.*
14. *Ibid.*
15. *Ibid.*
16. *Ibid.*
17. Coach and Lantern website, *www.coachandlantern.ca.*
18. Erin Rankin, "Hair-Raising Local Legend Lives On," *Ancaster News*, October 29, 2004.
19. *Ibid.*
20. *Ibid.*
21. *Ibid.*

SUGGESTED READING AND RESOURCES

During the course of conducting research for this book, I encountered a plethora of information about Hamilton's history as well as the haunted legacy the city has to offer. The information came in the form of books, resource centres such as libraries, and also the people who were delighted and willing to share their passion and what they knew.

Though I have likely not been successful in capturing every single useful resource that I encountered, I attempted to compile a list of the ones that I found myself fascinated with and which took me on delightful, sometimes divergent paths.

This is in no way an authoritative list of all the resources available for future research or study, but they are likely great places for you to start, should you want to explore various details or points covered in this book.

Books

Some of the books listed below are wide, encompassing sagas of Hamilton, its history, and its people, while others delve into details of one particular place, person, group, or circumstance. But one thing is certain: if you are at all interested in learning more about the Hamilton region, its history, and some of the interesting historical events and the people who shaped them, this suggested reading list would be a good place to start.

Anderson, Mary. *Tragedy & Triumph: Ruby & Thomas B. McQuesten*. Dundas: Tierceron Press, 2011.

Arnott, Kim, Ross Marvin, and Cherly MacDonald. *Hamilton Book of Everything*. Lunenberg: MacIntyre Purcell Publishing Inc., 2008.

Butts, Edward. *Murder: Twelve True Stories of Homicide in Canada*. Toronto: Dundurn Press, 2011.

Chapple, Nina. *A Heritage of Stone: Buildings of Niagara Peninsula, Fergus and Elora, Guelph, Region of Waterloo, Cambridge, Paris, Ancaster-Dundas-Flamborough, Hamilton and St. Marys*. Toronto: James Lorimer & Company Ltd., 2006.

Colombo, John Robert. *Ghost Stories of Ontario*. Toronto: Hounslow Press, 1995.

Elliot, James E. *Strange Fatality: The Battle of Stoney Creek, 1813*. Montreal: Robin Brass Studios, 2010.

Freeman, Bill. *Hamilton: A People's History*. Toronto: James Lorimer & Company Ltd., 2001.

Freeman Campbell, Marjorie. *A Mountain and a City: The Story of Hamilton*. Toronto: McClelland and Stewart, 1966.

The Head-of-the-Lake Historical Society. *Hamilton: Panorama of Our Past*. Hamilton: The Head-of-the-Lake Historical Society, 1994.

Henley, Brian. *Hamilton Our Lives and Times*. Hamilton: The Hamilton Spectator, 1993.

Houghton, Margaret. *Hamilton Street Names: An Illustrated Guide*. Toronto: James Lorimer & Company Ltd, 2002.

_____. *The Hamiltonians: 100 Fascinating Lives*. Toronto: James Lorimer & Company Ltd., 2003.

_____. *Vanished Hamilton*. Burlington: North Shore Publishing, 2005.

Italiano, Marcy. *Spirits and Death in Niagara*. Atglen: Schiffer Publishing Ltd., 2008.

Kosydar, Richard. *Hamilton: Images of a City*. Dundas: Tierceron Press, 1999.

Mott, A.S. *Haunted Schools: Ghost Stories and Strange Tales*. Edmonton: Ghost House Books, 2003.

Vallée, Brian. *Torso Murder: The Untold Story of Evelyn Dick*. Toronto: Key Porter Books, 2001.

WEBSITES

Adventures in Heritage (A blog by Kayla Jones)
www.adventuresinheritage.com

Kayla Jones is a young heritage professional based in southern Ontario. Her blog and website Adventures in Heritage shares her experiences in the heritage field. Her February 7, 2011, blog entry contains some interesting observations and impressions of Whitehern historic house (*www.adventuresinheritage.com/ blog/2011/02/whitehern-historic-house-highlights/*) and she has documented a fifty-two-week series of posts specifically about buildings in Hamilton.

Burlington Ghost Walks
www.burlingtonghostwalks.ca

Established in 1999, and a division of the Canada's Most Haunted media franchise, this website and group conduct investigations into Burlington and Halton Region's most haunted places.

Canada's Most Haunted is a research team that was founded

by director Patrick Cross in 2001. They specialize in spirit research and communication and work in both Canada and the U.S. with state-of-the-art equipment, which is regularly researched and updated. Their objective is to research anything that is deemed to be paranormal in nature, in the most accurate yet sensitive way possible. They use mediums as well as scientific exploration of the paranormal and never claim to have all the answers. The group welcomes the valuable input of their colleagues and will often seek it out as part of their investigations.

The team consists of director Patrick Cross, co-director Michelle Desrochers, and research team members Melissa McLennan and Tyler Mt. Pleasant. Nicole Sime is their administrator and Brian Wieland is the newest psychic consultant to join the team.

City of Waterfalls
www.cityofwaterfalls.ca

In the spring of 2008, Chris Ecklund decided to increase public awareness of a secret treasure known to only a few: its one-hundred-plus waterfalls. Up until that point, when one thought of Hamilton, one envisioned Stelco, McMaster University, the Tiger-Cats, or the Bulldogs. Except for locally famous falls like Webster's and Albion, the city's water resources were assumed to be limited to the harbour. The majority of Hamiltonians had no idea how many waterfalls and cascades danced and flowed within the city limits.

Ecklund, who was twice nominated for Citizen of the Year, sponsored the design and maintenance of the City of Waterfalls website. With its Facebook group, which is the largest on the Hamilton network, and highly interactive Keepers of the Water social network, the site has converted thousands of people into dedicated "waterfallers." Almost every weekend, Ecklund coordinates a waterfall walk. Webster's Falls, Hermitage Cascade, and the Devil's Punchbowl are among the locations visited so far. People have travelled from as far away as Chatham and Buffalo to participate. "I've spent about $100,000 on this venture, and I don't expect to get it back. I don't care about that," Ecklund told Werner. "This is about improving the image of Hamilton. This is something in our own backyard that we can promote to the world. We need to open the door and get people to see what we have."

Hamilton Conservation Authority
www.conservationhamilton.ca

Hamilton Conservation Authority, located at the western end of Lake Ontario, is the area's largest environmental management agency and is dedicated to the conservation and enjoyment of watershed lands and water resources. With a vision to ensure healthy streams and healthy communities in which human needs are met in balance with the needs of the natural environment, their mission statement is to lead in the conservation and enjoyment of watershed lands and water resources.

Hamilton Paranormal
hamiltonparanormal.com

Run between 1998 and 2005 by George and Cathy Brady, this website collected photos, stories, information, and history about various haunted locations in the Hamilton area.

Ontario Paranormal
ontarioparanormal.com

Ontario Paranormal is a website that shows the paranormal world in Ontario, Canada, and features places that can be visited through tours or on self-directed adventures. Whether rain or shine, this group looks beyond to find the unexplained through technology and reason.

This website includes photography taken by Mike C. Piccirillo for use in paranormal research and includes destinations and travel locations in Ontario, Canada. They state that the paranormal world and the unexplained is out there and that their website is dedicated to helping people understand the fact that we are not alone.

The Shadows Project
www.theshadowsproject.com

The Shadows Project is a group of individuals with a desire to learn about and understand the experiences that they and others consider paranormal. Throughout the years, they have visited popular locations with urban legends surrounding them and have been invited into people's homes to investigate reports of hauntings.

An Expeditions page on their website contains documented evidence and findings of all of their investigations. As a group, The Shadows Project understands there are no tools to detect ghosts and or spirit activity, yet they are willing to experiment with different devices both old and new to attempt to communicate with "ghosts."

The group makes no claims to mediumship or psychic ability and focus instead on their first-hand accounts of what they have encountered in their investigations.

Southern Ontario Paranormal Society
www.sopsinvestigations.com

SOPS was formed in October 2005 by Steve Genier as an extension of his ongoing research into the paranormal since 1996. Steve gathered other like-minded individuals to investigate claims of the paranormal with the common goal to network and provide a database to help further research into the vast unknown. Through non-profit means of investigating, and providing an outlet for those who seek to find some answers to a situation they don't understand, SOPS's continuous journey to uncover the great unknown is ever-growing. This is due to a very dedicated team. Their investigations cover most of Ontario and much of the U.S., and the group continuously works with others to ensure an open networking policy.

The Spectral Review
www.youtube.com/user/TheSpectralReview

Pictures, images, and video set to eerie music, many of which involve places in the Hamilton region that have paranormal activity associated with them.

Stableford, Michele (inactive website)

A renowned psychic medium living in Mount Hope, Ontario, Michele has used her gifts of clairvoyance, tarot, palmistry, and psychometry to help others in areas of love, career, and family for over twenty-five years, giving private readings from her home. She is also a certified Reiki master, giving healings and teaching this ancient Japanese technique. Michele has been able to see and communicate with "The Dead" since she was a little girl and has given messages from the spirit world to those who seek her guidance. Michele has been in the media (radio and television) investigating haunted locations or talking about her gifts as a psychic medium. She works with an investigation partner, Kim H. who is a psychic medium as well. Kim helps out using her psychic gifts during their many ghost investigations through Late Nite Haunts. Michele is the organizer/psychic of the many annual psychic fairs held at the Haunted Coach & Lantern British Pub in Ancaster, Ontario.

Link to interview with Michele by Daniel Cumerlato of Haunted Hamilton: *www.ghostwalks.com/20_article_destiny moon.html.*

The Hamilton Public Library
www.hpl.ca

The Hamilton Public Library (HPL) is a public library system that serves a population of more than 500,000 people in Hamilton, Ontario, with a single system consisting of twenty-four branches, thirty-four bookmobile stops, a virtual online branch, and a visiting library service for the homebound.

Other HPL services include the Local History and Archives Department (formerly called Special Collections), which houses an extensive collection of local history resources. In recent years, the HPL's collection of online resources has expanded rapidly, and now features more than thirty databases covering a great variety of topic areas.

Public libraries have operated in Hamilton since the 1830s, although the first branches were privately operated and tended to be ephemeral in nature. Hamilton city council voted to publicly fund the construction and operation of a library in 1889.

Hamilton was the first Canadian city to erect a new building for the express purpose of housing a library. An HPL branch opened on Hamilton's Barton Street in 1908. Andrew Carnegie funded a new main library, which opened in 1913. This was in turn replaced by a new, six-storey central library in 1980.

The *Hamilton Spectator*
www.thespec.com

Located at 44 Frid Street in Hamilton, the *Hamilton Spectator* (or the *Spec*, which it is affectionately known as) was first published

July 15, 1846. Since that date, it has been the voice of Hamilton and the surrounding area. Originally named the *Hamilton Spectator and Journal of Commerce*, the paper was founded by Robert Smiley and a partner, and was eventually sold in 1877 to William Southam, founder of the Southam newspaper chain. The *Spectator* was the first newspaper in the group, which grew from a single property to become a significant media voice in Canada for more than one hundred years.

OF RELATED INTEREST

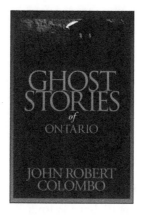

Ghost Stories of Ontario
by John Robert Colombo
978-0888821768
$16.99

Here is a book to thrill and chill you!
It brings together sixty-nine stories of haunted houses, ghosts, poltergeists, apparitions, and other eerie events and experiences.

- Did Sir John A. Macdonald give advice from beyond the grave?
- Does a beautiful lady in white haunt old stone houses in the north Woodstock area?
- What was behind the Baldoon Mystery and the Dagg Poltergeist?

In these pages there are ghosts aplenty. They appear in the villages, towns, and cities of Ontario — among them: Goderich, Hamilton, London, Toronto, Niagara-on-the-Lake, North Bay, Oakville, Oshawa, St. Catharines, and Sarnia! Perhaps there is a ghost near you....

Ghosts of the Canadian National Exhibition
by Richard Palmisano
978-1554889747
$24.99

When one thinks of Toronto's Canadian National Exhibition, memories of bright lights, cotton candy, the rush of people, and the excitement of rides spring to mind. But when the lights go down and the people head home, the fairground takes on a life of its own. The spirits that dwell there from the exhibition's long history come out to play and work, even to scare the occasional employee.

DUNDURN
www.dundurn.com

Visit us at
Dundurn.com
Definingcanada.ca
@dundurnpress
Facebook.com/dundurnpress